MW00713652

MARRIAGE WORKS!

To: Christian + Kim

With warmest best wishes!

E. Pendley

MARRIAGE WORKS!

Before You Say "I Do"

Elisabeth Pendley

Merril Press
Bellevue, Washington

MARRIAGE WORKS!

Copyright © 2006 by Elisabeth Pendley
ALL RIGHTS RESERVED. NO PART OF THIS BOOK MAY BE REPRODUCED IN ANY FORM OR BY ANY ELECTRONIC OR MECHANICAL MEANS INCLUDING INFORMATION STORAGE AND RETRIEVAL SYSTEMS WITHOUT WRITTEN PERMISSION, EXCEPT IN THE CASE OF BRIEF QUOTATIONS EMBODIED IN CRITICAL ARTICLES AND REVIEWS.

First Edition
Published by Merril Press

Typeset in Times New Roman by Merril Press, 12500 N.E. 10th Place, Bellevue, Washington 98005. Telephone 425-454-7009. Fax 425-451-3959. ISBN 13: 978-0-936783-46-8. E-mail address: books@merrilpress.com. Website: www.merrilpress.com. Cover design by Northwoods Studio.

Marriage Works! is distributed by Merril Press, P.O. Box 1682, Bellevue, Washington 98009. Additional copies of this book may be ordered from Merril Press at $16.95 each. Website www.merrilpress.com. Phone 425-454-7009.

LIBRARY OF CONGRESS CATALOGING-IN-PUBLICATION DATA

Pendley, Elisabeth, 1945
Marriage works : before you say "I do" / Elisabeth Pendley. -- 1st ed.
p. cm.
Includes bibliographical references and index.
ISBN 0-936783-46-X
1. Marriage counseling. 2. Mate selection. 3. Man-woman relationships. I. Title.

HQ10.P44 2006
646.7'7-de22

2006041915

PRINTED IN THE UNITED STATES OF AMERICA

Table of Contents

Table of Contents

Introduction

The definition of marriage is no mere policy issue. We're talking about the very integrity and meaning of one of the primary elements of civil society. For years, I have spoken and written about the numerous attacks on this important institution: welfare rules that undermine the family; the attempts of same-sex advocates to deconstruct marriage, the lack of a constitutional amendment to protect marriage between a man and a woman; the dangers pornography poses for the family and for children. Without question, these attacks on traditional marriage and family life constitute one of the most perilous developments of modern times.

For thousands of years, every society and every major religious faith have held that marriage is a unique relationship by which one man and one woman are joined together for the primary purpose of forming and maintaining a family. Today our society faces serious threats to this basic institution. Divorce has undermined family life and weakened our social structure. As a result of America's rampant divorce rate, more than one million children per year are involved in divorce; more than eight million children are now living with a divorced single parent. The decline in marriage is accompanied by other serious social problems such as the dramatic rise in the number of children born out of wedlock. These children are more likely to encounter poverty, welfare, physical abuse, behavioral and emotional problems, sexually transmitted diseases, lower educational achievement, drug and alcohol abuse, crime and imprisonment.

If we care about the very fabric of our society, we must take action to support the institution of marriage. However, this is not a matter for public policy alone nor is there some magic governmental solution. It is time that all elements of society support a culture and a social infrastructure to help couples prepare for a lifetime marriage. It is time that words like 'until death do us part" become meaningful again.

Lis Pendley has made a magnificent contribution to this effort with *Marriage Works! Before You Say "I Do"*. She believes, as do I, that couples must know each other well before they marry. In the vernacular of this book, couples are repeatedly asked: "Is this your best choice?" Numerous questions and stories from hundreds of dating and married couples tackle such issues as family relationships, in-laws, money, religious and ethnic differences, expectations, employment, sex, children and blended families. The goal? To find a life mate. At a time when expectations for a successful marriage are at an all time low, and couples engage in 'catch and release' relationships, this book will guide them through difficult issues. If the questions are answered seriously, secrets will be dispelled. And if the common sense advice given in *Marriage Works!* is heeded, couples will be equipped with the insight necessary to make their marriage successful.

Lis has performed a valuable and farsighted service by illuminating simple truths necessary for lasting relationships, truths that are too often ignored in our politically correct, non-judgmental, media-driven culture. *Marriage Works! Before You Say "I Do"* will help society to move forward, on a couple by couple basis, to reinstate commitment, compatibility, and communication into the institution of marriage.

Edwin Meese III
Washington, D.C.

Author's Preface

My family has given me a nickname, the "V.O.R.," which stands for the "Voice of Reason." Over the years, the V.O.R. has insisted on always wearing a helmet when riding a bike, on attending drivers' training classes before driving down our narrow mountain roads, and on eating pounds of vegetables.

Once my sons started to date, I focused on the issues faced by dating couples, including a skyrocketing divorce rate. I worried about the lack of commitment to marriage and the lowered expectations of relatives and friends.

And just as the V.O.R. has protected her sons in the past, I decided to give them a handbook on how to find their lifetime mate. So, *Marriage Works! Before You Say "I Do"* was written. This book contains questions that must be answered before marriage, stories from the many married and divorced people who shared their experiences with me, and finally, advice from the V.O.R.

I dedicate this book to my sons, W. Perry and Luke for whom this book was written.

Most specifically, I wish to thank my husband, Perry, who is my lifemate, my dearest friend, and my source of courage. Without his continued support, this book would not have been written.

Like all books, *Marriage Works!* is the product of many hands. I am deeply grateful to those who shared their most heartfelt experiences with me. Their stories are the core of this book!

In particular, I wish to thank my dearest friends and relatives who spent hours discussing this topic with me and giving me their advice.

My thanks to Alan M. Gottlieb of Merril Press, who accepted my manuscript for publication and to Ron Arnold, editor-in-chief of Merril Press, for his unending patience with me and for his yeoman duty guiding my book through the intricate production process.

Since this book was written, my son W. Perry has married Blair, a most remarkable young lady. I am now blessed with a daughter!

Whatever merits this book may have belongs to these fine people. Any errors of fact or judgment are mine alone.

Elisabeth Pendley
Evergreen, Colorado

Chapter 1

Your Best Choice?

At the time of the wedding, one bride had "hers" and "his" monograms etched on the gift of heirloom pewter candlesticks so that there would be no arguing over the gift when they divorced.

At another wedding reception, relatives of the bride commented that the groom was a darling fellow who would make a perfect "starter" husband for their niece.

No surprise, both of these marriages ended in divorce!

Most couples marrying today are aware that up to fifty percent of first marriages will fail with even higher divorce rates for second marriages.

Cohabiting before marriage is no protection from divorce; cohabiting couples face divorce rates higher than those who do not live together before marriage.

Studies now show that divorce is hazardous to health, with divorced women losing significantly more work time to illness and injury than married women.

On average, divorce lowers the standard of living, with a shocking thirty-eight percent of children of divorced parents living at or below poverty level.

Divorce profoundly affects the children. Children of divorce are more apt to suffer from poor school performance, drug abuse, sexual promiscuity, teen pregnancy, and suicide.

Recent studies have also shown that children are more at risk for abuse from live-in boyfriends and stepfathers than their natural fathers.

And finally, children of divorce are more likely to divorce as adults.

No one doubts that divorce has a lasting emotional, physical, and economic impact on the divorcing couple, the children, and society at large.

While numerous books are written on "how to fix" a troubled marriage, very few are written on how to avoid a troubled marriage to begin with.

Marriage Works! offers stories, questions and advice to help you evaluate your marriage success before you marry. Based on the premise that an in-depth knowledge of Your Beloved and the future in-laws will insure your marriage success, I now offer you my first piece of advice: sit down with Your Beloved, answer the questions, read the stories and discuss the issues raised in this book.

There isn't any reason to hurry through these chapters; you are building a relationship to last a lifetime.

So let's begin.
Is this your best choice?

When you daydream about finding Your Beloved, what do you wish for?

> My top requirements for a husband were (1) kind, (2) very intelligent, (3) excellent sense of humor, and (4) religious tolerance. My husband of thirty years has all of these characteristics.
>
> — Jean

List your expectations in order of importance, beginning with the most important:

1.

2.

3.

4.

5.

6.

7.

8.

9.

10.

Does Your Beloved meet all ten of these wishes?

If not, which ones are missing? Be honest. List them!

1.

2.

3.

4.

5.

How important are the missing expectations?

Are you planning to change Your Beloved to suit your expectations?

Assume that you can't change Your Beloved. Is he or she still your best choice?

> I really believe that "what you see is what you get!" If he drinks too much before you get married, or can't hold a job, or is too critical, or his mother is a pill, then that's what you have after you get married. Don't plan on changing anything!
>
> — Betty

How lasting are the characteristics you are seeking?

Are the qualities or characteristics enhanced by the passage of time?

And since this is a lifetime commitment, are these qualities and expectations going to be important to you twenty or thirty years from now?

If those characteristics were erased, would it matter to you?

> I wanted gorgeous, sexy, wealthy, and fun. I got it! After a few years, he gained weight, lost hair, and filed for bankruptcy. I filed for a divorce.
>
> — Alma

Where did you meet Your Beloved?

School? Work? Church? Through friends or relatives? Personal ad? Internet? Vacation? Singles bar? Exercise club?

How long have you known Your Beloved?

How long have you been seriously dating? Days? Months? Years?

It takes time to achieve a stable relationship, a relationship that will survive the inevitable conflicts of married life.

> All my life I searched for her, a beautiful brainy woman. After dating for six months, I married her. If I had spent more time courting her...if I had met her parents before we married...if I had paid attention to all the clues I refused to see...I never would have married her!
>
> — Steven

> We were intimate on the first date and married a few weeks later. What a mistake!
>
> — Molly

To avoid surprises, have you taken all the time you need to know Your Beloved before you marry?

> I knew she had been married before ...once before... but actually it was twice before. I was her third husband.
>
> — Mike

> I met and married him in less than three months. I married a stranger.
>
> — Cindy

> She was slim and energetic. I thought it was because she ate well and exercised; after we were married I learned that she had bulimia for years.
>
> — Hal

> After we got married, I realized that he needed a drink or two or three or more just to get through the day, every day!
>
> — Mary

> She was five months pregnant when we got married in a formal church wedding. I didn't know that the baby wasn't mine.
>
> — Jim

> He was so very shy and respectful when we were courting. There was handholding and a few chaste kisses. I was so very young and inexperienced. After marriage, I learned that my husband was a homosexual.
>
> — Judy

The questions in this book must be answered honestly in order to help you find and marry Your Beloved, your best choice, your best friend, your lover, your life mate.

To begin with, is Your Beloved your best choice?

Have you dated numerous others, and fallen into and out of love several times?

Have you dated others and known they were not your best choice?

Is your life "settled" and are you mature enough to make a lifetime commitment?

Why do you want to get married?

Check those reasons that apply to you:

- ☐ Your parents are pressuring you to settle down.
- ☐ All your friends are getting married.
- ☐ You have an unpleasant home life and you want to escape.

- ☐ You believe that Your Beloved will be a career asset.
- ☐ You believe that Your Beloved will be less expensive than maid service and carry out.
- ☐ Your biological clock is ticking and you want children.
- ☐ You are tired of the dating scene or of being alone.
- ☐ You're bored and want a change.
- ☐ You're in debt and need financial help.
- ☐ You believe that marriage will make you happy.
- ☐ You want to be a U.S. citizen.
- ☐ Your Beloved is already the parent of your child.
- ☐ Your Beloved is your best friend.
- ☐ You are living with Your Beloved and want to make it legal.
- ☐ You believe that Your Beloved is your life mate.
- ☐ You have already spent so many years on this relationship that it would be a waste of all that time not to get married.

If you are getting married because "no one else will ask me" or because "if it doesn't work out, I'll just get a divorce" or because "all my friends are getting married" or because "the invitations have been sent out and the dress has been bought and the honeymoon is paid for," stop right now!

These are not good reasons for getting married.

Being lonely, lustful, in love with love, in a hurry, in an unpleasant situation is not enough.

This is the most important, life changing decision you will ever make.

You can go back to school, change your career, move to another city, buy or sell your car or your house.

None of those decisions (important as they are) begin to equal your decision to marry.

This decision will affect you, Your Beloved, and your families forever.

Chapter 2

Know These Basic Facts

How well do you know Your Beloved?

> I spent more time deciding on the perfect dog for the family than I did choosing my husband. You know, one kid had allergies, so the dog couldn't shed and the yard was small so the dog couldn't be very big and the kids were rambunctious so the dog had to like roughhousing. I even read dog books on the "perfect dog for you" and I borrowed dogs to try them out. My husband? I only knew him a short time before we eloped. I was young, tired of being at home, and I thought I was "in love." I hadn't met his parents and really didn't know him very well. It didn't take long to figure out I had made a big mistake.
>
> —Ellie

Without asking, can you list some information about Your Beloved? Then fill in a list about you.

Very basic information about Your Beloved:

Name
Age
Height and Weight
Hair and Eye Color
Ethnic Background
Educational Background
Occupation
Religion
Political Affiliation
Parents: Married or Divorced
Names of Siblings

Very basic information about you:

Name
Age
Height and Weight
Hair and Eye Color
Ethnic Background
Educational Background
Occupation
Religion
Political Affiliation
Parents: Married or Divorced
Names of Siblings

Are there similarities and differences between Your Beloved and you on this basic information list?

What are the similarities?

1.

2.

3.

4.

5.

What are the differences?

1.

2.

3.

4.

5.

Do you have a similar educational background?

Have you both completed high school? College? Graduate school?

Do you have a similar ethnic or religious background?

Are there more differences than similarities?

If there are more differences than similarities, how will this affect your married life?

Are you prepared to work through these differences, adopt a new culture or religion, bridge an age gap?

Will you value these differences or resent them?

Will the differences cause more difficulty as your marriage progresses?

Less basic information about Your Beloved:

Can you answer all these questions without asking?

Check your answers with Your Beloved.

1. Middle name
2. Birthday
3. Favorite relative and why
4. The name of Your Beloved's childhood pet
5. The names of all siblings from oldest to youngest
6. The name and city of Your Beloved's high school
7. His or Her worst subject in high school/college
8. The names of two of Your Beloved's friends
9. Your Beloved's favorite sport

10. The name of the last movie seen
11. The most despised food
12. The worst experience of his/her life (so far)

> I was asked four questions by my mother when told that I had met a very special someone: What color are her eyes? What is her middle name? And (because her middle name was her grandmother's maiden name) is this her first marriage? And what was her astrological sign? I could answer three of the questions...I didn't know what color her eyes were!
>
> —Paul

> After being told that I really liked a fellow who was on scholarship at college and 6'5" tall, my mom's only question was an ethnic one, "Is he white?"
>
> —Hannah

> I married my high school sweetheart. I knew everything about him and his family.
>
> —Ruth

> We dated for two and one-half years before we were married. There were no surprises.
>
> —Ted

> I thought we knew each other really well. When we went to prenuptial counseling, I answered more than half the questions differently than my fiancé. I was crushed! After a lot more time together and constant prayer, we were finally ready to get married.
>
> —Anna

Is Your Beloved an optimist? Or a pessimist? What are you?

Outside of Hollywood, can an optimist and a pessimist live happily ever after?

> I am an optimist. Albert is a pessimist. I never worry about consequences; Albert worries about everything!
>
> —Jane

> Before I left on a European trip, he crashed every plane, derailed every train, and sunk every boat. After paint-

ing a catastrophic picture, he asked if I still wanted to go. I did! No trip could be as bad as he described.

—Victoria

Every headache is a brain tumor!

—James

Because he is a pessimist, he is always pleasantly surprised when things work out.

—Abby

Are you or Your Beloved a morning lark, a night owl, or both?

What happens when a night owl and a morning lark marry?

I had to go to bed when he did even if I weren't tired. He said I woke him up if I came to bed later. Reading in bed wasn't possible because the light bothered him. So I'd lie there and listen to him snore.

—Angie

I only need five hours of sleep at night; he needs eight to ten. I am a morning lark and he is a night owl. We just follow our own sleep schedule.

—Marty

She was a grouch in the morning before she had two or three cups of coffee. I promised her that I would never talk to her in the mornings before she drank her coffee, and that I would not sing during my morning showers.

—Henry

He often worked late. Even with no job outside the home and a full-time housekeeper, I was too tired to wait up for him. He promised not to wake me up when he crawled into bed at midnight or 1:00 A.M.

—Susan

What if Your Beloved is both a night owl and a morning person?

Are you a couch potato and Your Beloved the energizer bunny?

> No one can keep up with him. I no longer try!
>
> —Gail

Is it better if both of you are couch potatoes or both energizer bunnies?

Does it matter to you?

> We both read hundreds of books each year. A shared evening for us is sitting together reading, sipping tea, occasionally glancing up at the fire and each other.
>
> —Jack and Nancy

> We hike together, ride motorcycles or horses together, fly planes together, travel to foreign countries together, and entertain together. We constantly hustle ... together.
>
> —Neil and Nadine

> I run miles each week. My wife is plump and allergic to exercise.
>
> —Brad

After answering these questions, the basic similarities or differences between yourself and Your Beloved will be very obvious. The more compatible you both are (age, ethnic background, religion, political affiliation), the stronger the basis for your relationship will be. If there are more differences than similarities, you must discuss these differences now and determine how to make your marriage last a lifetime in spite of them.

In order to learn the answers to the basic questions asked in this chapter, it will be necessary to spend time with Your Beloved, to share experiences and to listen to each other's stories.

I believe that couples who want to build a lasting relationship must first know each other very well.

Take all the time necessary to fall in love.

Marrying someone after dating only a few weeks or months is marrying a stranger!

Chapter 3

Your Lifelong Partner

Many couples declare that they married because they were "in love." The state of being "in love" may be fleeting or it may last a lifetime.

What about your love? Check all the questions below that apply to you:

Are you in love?

Are you in love with being in love?

Do you think that this is too good to be true?

Do you think Your Beloved is too good for you?

Do you think of Your Beloved all the time?

Do you want Your Beloved to be the parent of your children?

Do you plan to grow old with Your Beloved?

Will Your Beloved meet all your needs and expectations?

Is Your Beloved your life preserver?

Do you plan to change your life (your career, your hairdo, your religion, your car, your clothes) to please Your Beloved?

Do you feel jealous or insecure when Your Beloved talks to others more attractive than you are?

Are you blissfully happy?

Does Your Beloved make you feel cherished? Special? More alive? Anxious? Self-conscious? Uncomfortable? Inadequate?

Do you want to share your thoughts, impressions, and visions for the future with Your Beloved?

Are you constantly worried that Your Beloved will leave you?

Or that there are other loves in Your Beloved's life?

Do you or Your Beloved make comparisons with past loves?

Do you practice writing your married name?

Do you look forward to spending time with Your Beloved, even doing activities that are not your favorites?

Do you think Your Beloved is sexy?

Do you enjoy the physical expressions of your love?

Is physical love the only love you share?

Do you feel trapped? Grateful? Scared to commit?

Do you feel confident that Your Beloved is firmly committed to you?

> Thirty-two years ago, an elderly pastor read these words during our wedding ceremony: "Love is patient, love is kind. It does not envy, it does not boast, it is not proud. It is not rude, it is not self-seeking, it is not easily angered, it keeps no record of wrongs. Love does not delight in evil but rejoices with the truth. It always protects, always trusts, always hopes, always perseveres. Love does not fail." (1 Corinthians 13:4-8)
>
> —Will and Beth

Can you say this about Your Beloved?

Will Your Beloved say this too?

If you can't, what is missing?

Describe your experiences with Your Beloved that support your conclusion.

Are you prepared to spend a lifetime without this kind of love?

Are you willing to put this marriage prospect aside and seek your Best Choice?

While being in love is important, being "in like" is equally important. Many of the happily married couples who answered the questionnaire insisted that the most important aspect of their marriage was their deep friendship.

Are you "in like"?

Is Your Beloved your best friend?

If there is a problem or a triumph, is Your Beloved the first person you talk to?

Do you trust Your Beloved?

Do you respect Your Beloved and listen to his or her opinions?

Does Your Beloved listen to your opinions?

Do you believe that Your Beloved wants only the best for you?

Do you have many shared memories that you remember fondly?

Do you feel proud of Your Beloved's achievements?

Do you discuss ideas, books, movies, and events?

Do you discuss the people in your life-family, friends, co-workers, acquaintances?

Do you feel that you have to agree with Your Beloved, even if you don't?

Does Your Beloved become hostile if you don't agree?

Have you argued with Your Beloved and resolved the arguments fairly?

Do you share common interests, hobbies, and background?

If you weren't in love with Your Beloved, would you still be "in like"?

> You've got to have more than sex. You've got to be friends too. So when sex is less important, there is something more.
>
> —Ted

> I met him through music, a shared interest. He is my friend, my lover, my protector, my guide, my spiritual advisor, and my soul mate. I can't imagine life without him.
>
> —Roberta

He is my best friend. There isn't anything we can't talk about. I trust him completely and I know that he trusts me!

—Sharon

He is my husband, not my friend. When I try to talk to him, he says, why don't you call one of your girlfriends?

—Martha

My drinking buddies are my friends, not the old ball and chain.

—John

Feelings of jealousy, envy, insecurity, or hostility do not belong in a marriage of two compatible, committed adults. If you are experiencing negative feelings rather than love, stop now and reevaluate your future with Your Beloved. This isn't your best choice.

While deep feelings of love are the foundation for a lifetime marriage, it is equally important to like Your Beloved. You should be best friends.

A solid friendship is the most important ingredient in a successful marriage.

Chapter 4

Set Your Priorities

How do you arrange these lifetime priorities?
(A) Family, (B) Friends, (C) Religion/Philosophy, (D) Work.

List them by importance, most important first:

1.

2.

3.

4.

How does Your Beloved arrange these same priorities?

1.

2.

3.

4.

If you list "work" as number one and Your Beloved lists "family" as number one, will this affect your decision to marry or your married life?

> My mom always wanted me to marry a doctor. You know, the prestige thing. I think she wanted to be able to say, "My son-in-law the doctor says..." So I did. He's never around.
>
> —Deborah

Or what if Your Beloved lists "religion" as number one and you list it as number four? Is this a problem?

> I am seriously dating a woman who goes to church every Sunday. I play golf every Sunday. She doesn't play golf at all. The last times I went to church were for my brother's wedding and my mom's funeral.
>
> —Bill

> I married a good man and we have a good marriage but he is not the spiritual leader in our home. I miss not being able to have religious discussions with him.
>
> —Julia

I firmly believe that the lifetime priorities that you and Your Beloved share should be similar.

Being alone isn't lonely but being in a relationship in which your lifetime goals are not similar is very lonely. You may be the work widow, or you may have to be the sole supporter of your family; you may attend religious services alone or you may feel left behind when your spouse seeks comfort in religion; you may be embraced in a loving family or you may be estranged from your family; you may be encircled with friends or you may be friendless.

Ethnic, economic, or educational differences may cause friction, but the absence of similar lifetime goals will endanger your relationship.

Consider Your Beloved carefully; is this your best choice?

Chapter 5

To Have and to Hold ... Equally!

Are you equals? Competitors? Friends?

Do you both have the same level of self-confidence and self-esteem?

Are either of you "giving up" something to make this relationship work?

Does this relationship enhance both of your lives?

> She is an Anglo language teacher. I am a Hispanic railroad engineer. She loves books, poetry, politics, and art. I love hunting, fishing and smoking cigars. She's Episcopalian; I'm Catholic. After twenty years and two children, we are divorced.
>
> —James

> I am a talkative partygoer; he is a quiet loner. He's just there; I call him, "the wallpaper."
>
> —Angela

> I am college educated and the treasurer of a large corporation. He is an out-of-work carpenter who adores me. I married him.
>
> —Helen

> He always had to make all the decisions: the baby's name, which house or car we bought, who we voted for, what church we attended, where we took vacations. He controlled everything. If I disagreed, he was furious.
>
> —Rhoda

> He didn't like my hair, my makeup, or my clothes. He didn't even like my name. He refused to call me by my first name and used my middle name instead.
>
> —Kris

A lifetime relationship must be a relationship of equals. The relationship must enhance both of your lives. You should not have to give up your family, your desire for children, your religion, your friends, or your career to make it work.

In a relationship of equals, both voices will be heard and all opinions expressed without fear. Compromise isn't always possible; however, in a committed relationship, you can agree to disagree.

Your Beloved should enhance your life, as you are right now, not force you to change your life to fit his or her life. If you are going to have to change significantly to make this relationship work, this isn't your best choice.

Chapter 6
Common Grounds

Hollywood scoffs at the need for compatibility. The box office demand for a happy ending reinforces the popular myth that opposites attract and smitten couples will live happily ever after.

Numerous movies pair old and young, white and black, liberal and conservative, rich and poor, confident and insecure, Catholic, Protestant, Jewish or atheist, and ethnically diverse. The movie credits roll and we are left to conclude that the relationship endures. But, outside the movie theater, as most people realize, *compatibility* in a committed marriage is essential.

Even aspiring short-term roommates (summer camp or college dorms) fill out questionnaires to determine compatibility: messy or neat? smoker or nonsmoker? rock music or classical? night owl or morning lark? The more compatible the roommates are, the fewer issues become confrontational.

The 1995 romantic comedy, *Forget Paris*, addresses the compatibility of a state-side basketball referee, Mickey Gordon, and Paris-based airline customer relations executive Ellen Andrews, characters played by Billy Crystal and Debra Winger.

At one point, miserable, separated by the Atlantic Ocean and their careers, Ellen decides to join Mickey unexpectedly at his motel room.

As sweetly romantic music plays in the background, the questions begin, as I've transcribed for you here from a video:

> ELLEN: Do you sleep with the window open?
> MICKEY: Uh . . . yeah.
> ELLEN: I don't like it, you're going to have to stop that.
> MICKEY: Okay. Do you squeeze the toothpaste from the top or the bottom?
> ELLEN: Uh . . . top.
> MICKEY: Well don't do that, I hate that.
> ELLEN: If you ever use my car, you better put the mirror and the seat back where I like them.
> MICKEY: Don't use my razor to shave any part of you.
> ELLEN: If you ever start to lose your hair, you better not grow that big long thing down from your side burn, and wrap around your head, because it's disgusting and I don't like that.
> MICKEY: Don't ever hand me food and say, "Taste this, see if it's bad."
> ELLEN: All right.
> MICKEY: Okay.
> ELLEN: Want to talk about religion, politics, whether you want to have kids or not?
> MICKEY: Nah, that crap will work itself out. We've handled the big issues.
> ELLEN: All right, I'll marry you.

Copyright © 1995 Columbia Pictures

This, of course, is light comedy, but it's an intelligent parody of what really happens to many unwary couples. It's intelligent because "that crap," the stuff that couples refuse to discuss before they get married since it's awkward or embarrassing or might cause a fight, is the reason so many marriages end in divorce.

This unrealistic happy-ending movie is gently reminding us of a stark reality: that if you do not discuss the most essential elements in your marriage, you will marry a stranger. You will be lacking the communication skills needed to discuss a lifetime of issues. You will be unsure of Your Beloved's commitment to your marriage.

Love is blind. I so wanted him to be the right one!

—Leslie

I knew there was a lot we didn't discuss. Finances were the biggie. (I thought he had a lot of money; actually he was heavily in debt!) I was afraid if I mentioned it, he would get angry, or think I was only interested in his money and call off the wedding.

—Wendy

I knew she was proud of being a high-powered career woman. But I thought all women wanted children. After we got married I was shocked when she refused to start a family.

—Henry

I knew he was close to his mom but I never dreamed that she would move in with us after we got married. I never asked.

—Megan

Even though all his relatives lived in Iran, I never thought he would want to go back there to teach. After our two boys were born, he told me to pack their things. He was taking them home to be raised in the family. I wasn't invited!

—Allison

Before I ever marry again, I will hire a private detective, call the credit bureau, check his employment record, insist on a physical and an AIDS test, talk to his friends, meet his siblings and parents, attend a year of prenuptial counseling and get answers for all the questions in this book! Did I forget anything?

—Maggie

In order to avoid surprises, to know Your Beloved, to determine just how compatible you both are now and will be in the future, to determine how well you communicate and how great is your commitment to this marriage, you must answer these questions truthfully. If you pretend to like something, you may be sentencing yourself to eating sushi, listening to train music, and living with his or her mom for the rest of your married life.

This isn't a weekend fling or a job interview. This is your search for a life mate, your best choice.

Just how compatible are you and Your Beloved?

Likes	You	Your Beloved
Favorite dinner?		
Favorite dessert?		
Favorite drink?		
Favorite music?		
Favorite movie?		
Favorite book?		
Favorite sport?		
Favorite exercise?		
Favorite pet?		
Favorite spare-time activity?		
Favorite city?		
Favorite climate?		
Favorite vacation?		

Dislikes	You	Your Beloved
Worst dinner?		
Worst dessert?		
Worst drink?		
Worst music?		
Worst movie?		
Worst book?		
Worst sport?		
Worst exercise?		
Worst pet?		
Worst spare-time activity?		
Worst city?		
Worst climate?		
Worst vacation?		

> Thirty years ago, my husband quizzed me on our first date. Here are his questions. Did I plan to graduate from school? Did I plan to work? Was I a Christian? Did I drink, smoke, like to party, ski or swim? Did I want a family? What were my favorite colors? What was my favorite music? My answers convinced him that he should marry me!
>
> —Patty

She told me she loved country and western music. After we were married, she tried to sell all my tapes at a garage sale. "Only low lives listen to country and western," she said.

—Dave

Before we married, she loved football, knew the plays and the names of the players. She never missed watching a game and bought tickets to a Broncos game as a special surprise. After we were married, she didn't have time to watch the games with me, forgot all the plays and the names of the players. Finally she admitted that she didn't like football. Now why did she do that?

—Jack

I met her jogging on the park trails. We spent months running together. We played tennis, skied, snorkeled and biked together. Most of our dates included physical exercise. After we married she refused to exercise with me. I couldn't believe it.

—Ted

Searching for common grounds is humorously explored in the 1993 romantic comedy, *Groundhog Day*, in which cynical TV weatherman Phil Connors (Bill Murray) is forced to continuously re-live the worst day of his life until he learns to become a better person and worthy of Rita (Andie MacDowell), his TV producer.

When Phil asks Rita to explain her perfect guy, we're treated to this dialog, which I transcribed for you from a video:

RITA: Well, first of all, he's too humble to know he's perfect.
PHIL: That's me.
RITA: He's intelligent, supportive, funny.
PHIL: Intelligent, supportive, funny; me, me, me.
RITA: He's romantic and courageous.
PHIL: Me also.
RITA: He's got a good body but he doesn't have to look in the mirror every two minutes.
PHIL: I have a great body and sometimes I go months without looking.
RITA: He's kind, sensitive and gentle. He's not afraid to cry in front of me.

PHIL: This is a man we're talking about, right?
RITA: He likes animals, children and he'll change poopy diapers.
PHIL: Does he have to use the word "poopy?"
RITA: Oh, and he plays an instrument and he loves his mother.
PHIL: Whew, I am really close on this one, really, really close.

Copyright © 1993 Columbia Pictures

I have never believed that there is only one Ms. or Mr. Right. Forcing Your Beloved into the "right person" mold is a bad idea.

Even your best choice won't be perfect, but, if you answer all these questions, you will know Your Beloved's shortcomings before you marry.

Do not ignore the clues that are apparent in every relationship simply because you are tired of dating and hope that this person is your life mate. Let your relationship grow slowly.

If after answering these questions, you determine this isn't your best choice, end the relationship and move on.

Chapter 7

Who Are You?

Another way to judge compatibility with Your Beloved is to take a personality test. There are numerous personality tests available, some much more structured than others are. Personality tests are helpful to understanding yourself and Your Beloved. The insights of these tests will color the picture you already have of Your Beloved; they will illuminate your similarities and differences.

The Meyers-Briggs Personality Test categorizes people as introvert or extrovert, sensing or intuitive, thinking or feeling, and perceiving or judging.

Gary Smalley and John Trent encourage couples to take a personality test in *The Two Sides of Love.* For example, the Personal Balance Point Test determines how "hard" or "soft" you/Your Beloved are.

The Lion-Otter-Beaver-Golden Retriever test allows you and Your Beloved to decide if you are a lion (take charge leader), an otter (fun seeking visionary), a beaver (rule follower) or a golden retriever (loyal listener and encourager).

MARRIAGE WORKS!

Chapter 8

Childhood Memories

Traits and characteristics from your childhood and your parents reappear in you, especially as you grow older and/or become a parent yourself.

Are your childhood and your family backgrounds compatible with those of Your Beloved?

Have you discussed your childhood with Your Beloved?

It is your childhood that has molded you into the person he or she loves. Sit down with Your Beloved and tell stories from your past. Show Your Beloved the family album. Yep, there you are with braces, the dumbest haircut in your life and a large bandage on your chin from falling against the coffee table. Aren't you adorable? Trust me, Your Beloved will think so.

Did you have a happy childhood?

What are your favorite childhood memories?

Are you the first born? Middle child? Baby?

Were you adopted? Do you know your birth parents?

Did your parents have a favorite child?

> Everything—money, clothes, expensive college, and car—was lavished on my older sister. I was ignored.
>
> —Jo

> I was the favorite! I was the Princess. None of the rules applied to me.
>
> —Andrea

Were you the favorite? Were you the scapegoat?

Did you have favorite brothers or sisters? Why?

Have you been told you are very much like a relative?

Did you have your own bedroom?

Did you have a job after school or during the summer?

Did you have an allowance? What were you expected to buy with your allowance?

Did you have your own television, stereo, telephone, and car?

Were any of your brothers or sisters disabled?

If so, how did this disability affect you and your family?

> My older brother was physically handicapped. He was included in everything. We were all very close.
>
> —Don

> My younger sister was mentally retarded. It put a strain on the entire family. She got all the attention and there was never any time or energy left for the rest of us.
>
> —Evelyn

Did any of your brothers or sisters die? What was the cause of death? How did this affect your family? You?

Were you ever very sick? What disease did you have?

Did you have any operations as a child? Why?

Did you have psychological or family counseling as a child? Why?

Were you ever in a serious accident as a child? How did it happen? What injuries did you have?

What current medical problems resulted from these childhood illnesses or accidents?

Have these medical problems been resolved?

> My twin sister was killed in a sledding accident. My parents never got over it. I always wondered if they wished it had been me instead.
>
> —Dorothy

> Their son committed suicide when he was a teenager. His room remained unchanged for years. His death blasted a huge hole in the family. Everyone blamed himself or herself for his suicide.
>
> —Molly

> I was only the fifth person in the country to have a complex heart operation. I know my parents "hovered" before the operation but afterwards they didn't treat me any differently from my brother. They never restricted me physically.
>
> —Paul

> My parents took me to a shrink because I wasn't doing very well in school. He was a real flake! All he talked about was sex and whether I had seen any porn films lately. What did that have to do with scholastic achievement?
>
> —Hank

Did you have household chores? What were they?

Were you a latch key child? How did you feel about being alone?

Were you in charge of the younger children?

How were you disciplined as a child?

Did your parents hit you, ground you, or take away privileges?

Were you physically, mentally or sexually abused as a child? If so, by whom?

Has that situation been resolved?

How has this abuse affected you?

Have you received counseling?

Did you have a pet dog, cat, bird, horse, hamster, fish or rat?

What were your pets' names?

Did you have more than one pet at a time?

Who took care of these pets?

Tell at least one story that involves a childhood pet.

Do you prefer dogs to cats? Cats to dogs?

Did you move several times when you were a child or did you stay in the same home?

If you moved, what was the reason for the move?

Did you enjoy moving or hate it?

What schools did you attend?

Were you a good student?

Did you have a favorite teacher?

Did you ever get in trouble at school? Why?

What awards did you win as a child?

Were you popular?

Did you have many friends?

Were you an overachiever or an underachiever?

What examples can you give?

What were your faults as a child? Your strengths?

What was the family position on alcohol, drugs, tobacco use?

Did you experiment with alcohol, drugs, or tobacco? How often?

Did your parents know that you experimented?

What happened when they found out?

What was the family position on religion?

Was the Bible or other religious text often read in your home?

Did you all attend religious services regularly?

Did either your mom or dad teach Sunday school, or serve on a religious board, or sing in the choir?

What was the worst thing that happened to you as a child? Why?

What was the best thing that happened to you as a child? Why?

Information about Your Beloved as a child will help you understand the person he or she has become and the family dynamics in which he or she was raised. This information, blended with your own childhood will help you imagine your family life together.

If Your Beloved had a happy childhood, treasured by his parents, raised with love and discipline, you can expect Your Beloved to model his or her family life with you on his or her own experiences.

However, economic hardship, illness, divorce, abuse, or death will also have affected Your Beloved's childhood and will affect your family life together.

If your childhood or Your Beloved's childhood was less than ideal, discuss these issues and decide how they might affect your family life together.

MARRIAGE WORKS!

Chapter 9

Parents

Were your mom and dad from different ethnic backgrounds?

> Dad met Mom overseas. She left her family and culture to come to America. She was very brave, don't you think?
>
> —Mei

Were your mom and dad from different religious backgrounds?

> Mom was a Catholic and Dad was a Jew. Dad agreed to raise the children Catholic, but he never went to church with us.
>
> —Rosalie

Did your grandparents or other relatives live with you? Did you have a favorite aunt or uncle? Why?

Did your mom and dad go to high school, college, graduate school?

> Neither of his parents finished grade school. Both of my parents finished college and graduate school. He was the first in his family to go to college!
>
> —Lorraine

What was your dad's occupation?

Did he work two jobs at one time?

My dad was a pipe fitter for the railroad and worked at the bowling alley at night. Her dad was an architect. I never felt comfortable with her parents.

—Allen

Did he travel a lot or work late often?

Did your dad ever quit or lose his job?

Did he change careers?

First Dad was a high-powered advertising executive, then he quit, went to seminary and now he is a hospice minister. His life was transformed but so was all of ours.

—Jean

Did he attend your school plays and sports events?

My parents never once watched me march in the school band.

—Suzy

My dad attended every basketball game. He scheduled his work around my games.

—Annie

What five words would you use to describe your dad?

Do these words describe you too?

Do you respect your dad?

Do you identify with your dad? Why?

Did your mom work outside the home?

Did your mom ever quit or lose her job?

Did she change careers?

My mom said she was "just a housewife" but to us she was much, much more. She was the listening ear! She always had cookies and milk with us when we got home from school.

—Doug

> My mom was a lawyer. She worked sixty hours a week. We had live-in nannies, live-out nannies, day care, all day kindergarten, early and late school. But she always had time to bake desserts and read us stories.
>
> —Bob

If she worked outside the home, did she travel a lot or work late often?

Did she belong to the PTA, attend school plays or sports events?

What five words would you use to describe your mom?
Do these words describe you too?
Do you respect your mom?
Do you identify with your mom? Why?

Who did the majority of the household chores?
What specific chores did your mom do? Your dad?
Were your parents satisfied with this arrangement?

Economically, were your parents poor, middle class, upper middle class, wealthy?

> My dad was a white-collar worker; hers was a blue-collar worker. We came from two different economic worlds.
>
> —James

Did your parents rent or own your home?
Did your parents own more than one car?

Was either of your parents very sick when you were a child?

Was either of your parents alcoholics, drug users, or mentally ill?

If so, did your parents receive treatment?
Does this condition continue now?
Was either of your parents handicapped?
How did this affect you and your family?

Do you remember your parents fighting?
What were the fights usually about?

Did they ever throw things at each other or hit each other when they fought?

Were the fights ever so bad that the police were called?
Was either of your parents jailed for domestic abuse?

Was either of your parents unfaithful?
Did you know about this as a child?
Were you asked to keep "the secret"?
How did this affect your childhood?

Did your parents divorce when you were a child?
Do you know why?
If so, how old were you when they divorced?
What did this divorce mean to you? A move? New home? New school? Less money? Absent dad or mom?
Did you have counseling to deal with this loss?
How do you feel about the divorce now?
Did either parent remarry?
Did you grow up in a blended family?
Did you live with your step-parent?
Did you like your step-parent, step-brothers or step-sisters?
Did you believe that you were treated fairly by your step-parent?

Did either of your parents die when you were a child?
If so, how old were you when this happened?
Did you receive any counseling to deal with this loss?

Look carefully at Your Beloved's parents. If your parents and Your Beloved's parents are similar in religious, economic, and ethnic backgrounds, members of a traditional marriage, you will be able to draw from similar childhood experiences.

These two people have shaped Your Beloved into the person you love. They are responsible for the color of his or her hair and eyes, height and intelligence, but they have also taught Your Beloved to trust, to love, and to have faith. They have imprinted mannerisms, expressions of speech, and work ethics. They have provided Your Beloved with a blueprint for the rest of his or her life.

If Your Beloved's parents were nurturing and caring, Your Beloved will reflect this. However, parents who are indifferent, cold, or actively hostile also make a lasting impression on a child. Your

Beloved is affected by this uncaring behavior. Discuss this with Your Beloved. When you are with his or her parents, look for examples of this treatment.

If Your Beloved is estranged from his or her parents and describes them negatively, it will take a major effort at reconciliation by both of you to change this difficult relationship. Consider carefully the problems this difficult relationship may cause your marriage. Discuss this with Your Beloved.

Parents with a history of absence, infidelity, addiction, or divorce create a chaotic family life and inflict trauma and pain on their children. These children have not experienced a nurturing family life and will have difficulty imagining one. And they will have a hard time understanding a commitment to a relationship when problems arise.

If this is Your Beloved's family experience, you will have to work with him or her to instill commitment to your marriage and to provide the guide for a normal family life. If you are unwilling to accept this additional responsibility, or Your Beloved is not committed to your relationship, this isn't your best choice!

MARRIAGE WORKS!

Chapter 10

Family Life

What did you do as a family?

Play cards and board games?
Play musical instruments? Sing?
Hike? Ski? Go camping?
Swim? Go biking? Do gardening?
Watch movies or television?
Go on picnics?
Fish? Hunt?
Go to church?
Go on vacations? Where?
Visit grandparents or family friends?
Anything else?

How did your family celebrate birthdays? Christmas? New Years? Fourth of July? Hanukkah? Passover? Kwanzaa?

What foods were eaten at the traditional holiday celebrations?

Did all your relatives celebrate together?

My Aunt Millie always drank too much, started arguments and stomped out of the house before dessert.

—Alice

We all gathered for a big meal on Thanksgiving. One year we ran out of turkey and all my uncle had left to eat was the turkey neck.

—Frances

Did you open your Christmas presents on Christmas Eve or Christmas Day?

He always opened Christmas presents after Christmas Eve church service and gifts from Santa were unwrapped. I completely disagreed; Santa delivered presents only on Christmas day, and all presents, even those from Santa, had to be wrapped! This took years to resolve.

—Jenny

Christmas to me was church and family. Christmas to him was presents, the latest movie, and restaurant food.

—Bertha

Mom was Jewish and Dad was Catholic. I thought I was really special because we celebrated both Christian and Jewish holidays. One year we hung dreidles on the Christmas tree!

—Kyle

Did you dye and hide Easter eggs?
Did you dress for Halloween? Did you trick or treat?

We decorated the entire house for Halloween. Grandma would tell fortunes; Grandpa was a ghost. There was a "coffin" in the dining room filled with soda, eerie music, a headless ghoul and piles of trick or treat candies for the neighborhood children. When I suggested this to my bride, she thought I was nuts!

—David

What were your family's birthday traditions?
Were you a "special" person for the day?
Did you have your favorite dinner and a birthday cake?

When I got married, I had to bake my own birthday cake. My mother-in-law gave both of us birthday presents on my birthday. She didn't want her son to feel "left out."

—Meredith

Only decade birthdays were celebrated. Every ten years there was a party!

—Harold

Birthdays were non-events. No one ever made a cake. No presents were bought or wrapped. Money was given.

—Samuel

Birthday presents were always what I needed: socks, underwear, and shirts. These were grudgingly given.

—Alma

Birthdays were a big deal! Birthday wishes were discussed for weeks. Presents were bought and wrapped. There were cards (even from the dogs), balloons, cake and ice cream and my favorite dinner.

—Grant

What other family traditions did you have that were not connected with special holidays or birthdays?

School snow days meant fires in the fireplace, and eating homemade cinnamon rolls or doughnuts.

—Jonathan

We fished every summer in a cold high mountain stream. We never caught any fish but we enjoyed the stark beauty and the serenity and we laughed about the cold.

—Rebecca

We always walked under the cherry blossoms every spring.

—Ryoko

Once every summer, we took a thermos of hot chocolate and drove up to the top of the mountain to watch the sunrise. It was like sitting on top of the world.

—Liza

We watched a lot of hockey games. Specific foods were eaten during each period: first period was hot dogs and fries, second period was peanuts, and third period was ice cream!

—Joe

We always spent a few days at the seashore every summer.

—Annie

Every 4th of July, we met at my aunt's summer cabin at the lake. It was potluck, so we ate for hours. Then we sang songs and played games.

—Louis

Will you be able to share your holiday traditions with Your Beloved?

Are there any differences between the way you celebrate and Your Beloved's traditions?

If there are differences, how do you plan to resolve them?

What were three favorite family sayings or expressions?

"Holy cow!" "Good grief!" "My word!" "Dear me!" topped our family list.

—Will

"You must be someone else's child because my children don't misbehave."

—Shirley

"Always take a book with you. It's amazing how many books you can read while you're waiting."

—Susan

"There's a lot of injustice in this world. You're bound to run into it sometime."

—Walter

"Don't ever be surprised at what people do. But you may sometimes be surprised at which people do those things."

—Lee

Family traditions, the way birthdays and special holidays are celebrated, give sparkle to your life together. Planning parties, hiding presents, bringing home flowers when it snows in May, or creating new traditions bind you more closely together.

It is the family celebrations that are remembered forever.

Chapter 11

The Family Tree

Fill in your Family Tree together. On the following two pages I've provided room to list the family trees of You and Your Beloved back to your great-grandparents.

It's just the beginning of a family genealogy, but it covers the family members you are most likely to know or to have known face to face or to be familiar with through photo albums and family stories.

After all the names are listed, add pertinent information, such as birth/death dates, siblings, number of children, medical history, occupations, ethnic background, religion.

Tell stories about your grandparents and great-grandparents.

What similarities are there between your parents and grandparents and Your Beloved's?

What differences?

Are there more similarities than differences?

The Family Tree

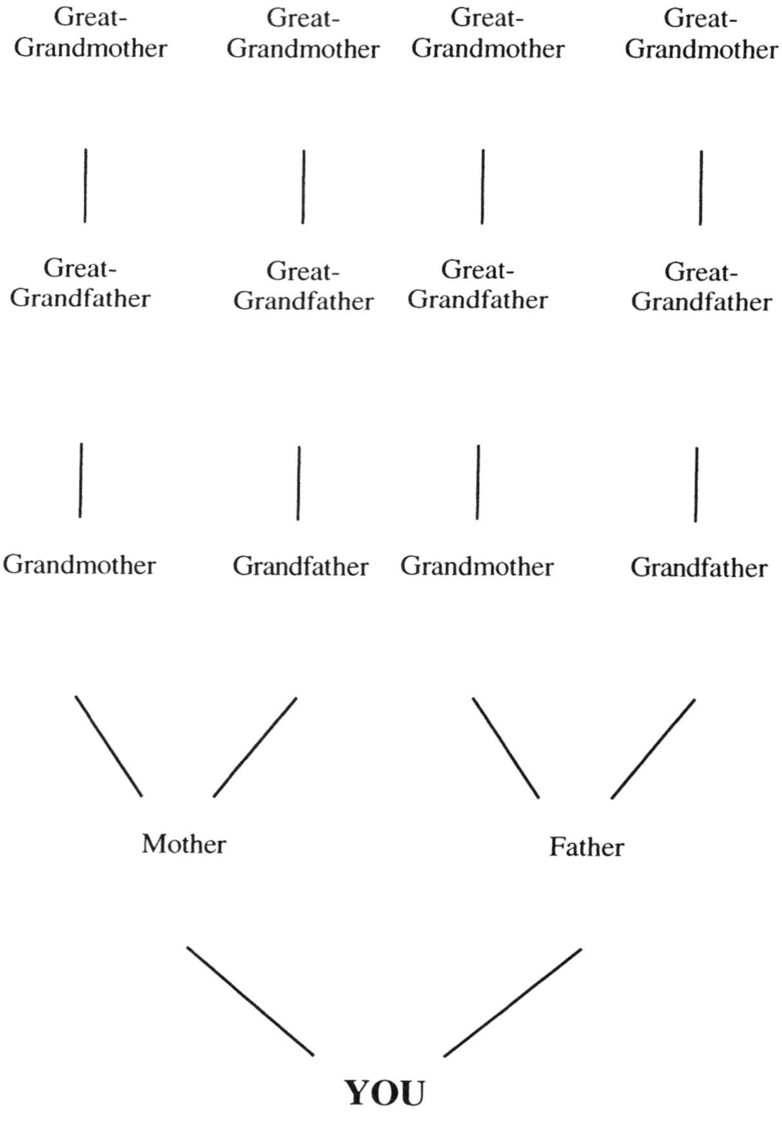
Great-
Grandmother
Great-
Grandmother
Great-
Grandmother
Great-
Grandmother
Great-
Grandfather
Great-
Grandfather
Great-
Grandfather
Great-
Grandfather
Grandmother
Grandfather
Grandmother
Grandfather
Mother
Father
YOU

The Family Tree

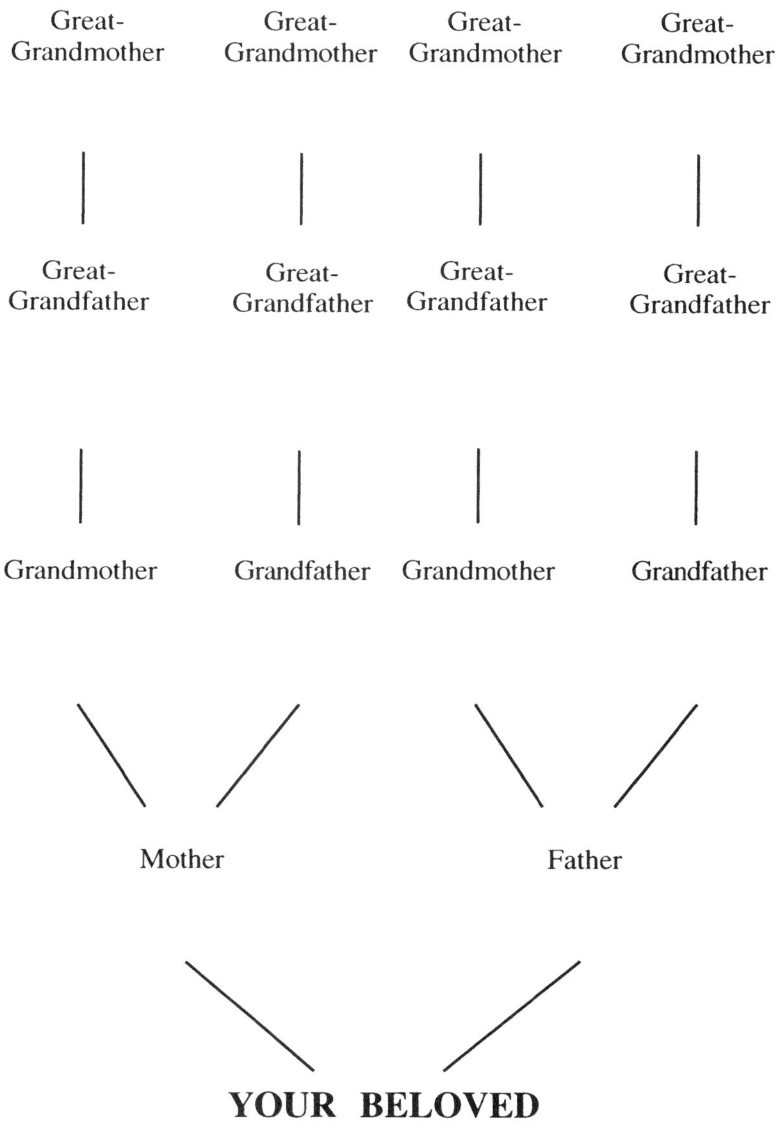

MARRIAGE WORKS!

Chapter 12

Mama's Boy? Daddy's Boy?

In Francis Ford Coppola's movie, *The Godfather* (Paramount Pictures © 1972), Michael Corleone (Al Pacino) tells his girlfriend, Kay Adams (Diane Keaton), a particularly brutal story about his father's business methods. When Kay looks shocked, Michael reassures her by saying, "That's my family, Kay. That's not me."

Not that you're likely to marry into a Mafia family or a movie family, but you will marry into somebody's family, and it's essential to know Your Beloved's parents.

Brides, look at your future father-in-law carefully.

Spend time with him alone.
Ask him questions about Your Beloved.
Notice the similarities between him and his son.
Is he willing to talk with you?
Do they look alike?
Do they have the same interests and values?
Are they in the same occupation or family business?
Does he speak about Your Beloved proudly?
Do they have the same personality or mannerisms?
Do they have the same sense of humor?

Is he in good health?

Does he love his wife and treat her with kindness and respect?

Does he attend religious services with his family?

Does he know what Your Beloved's interests and goals are?

Do you like him? Why or why not?

Can you tell if he likes you?

> He was very quiet. He really never spoke much at all. We would sit and have coffee and he would stir and stir and stir the sugar into his cup. It was so peaceful being with him. I always knew that he loved me.
>
> —Dana

Brides, look at your future mother-in-law carefully.

Spend time with her alone.

Perhaps without realizing it, Your Beloved will compare you with her. After all, she is his model of a wife and mother.

Was she a stay-home wife and mother or a career woman?

What are you planning to be?

> My mom was a housewife but his mom always worked. Since I planned on a career, I was glad she was a career woman too.
>
> —Janna

Ask her questions about being a wife and a mother.

In particular, ask questions about Your Beloved.

Does she speak about Your Beloved proudly?

> His mother always came first, no matter what!
>
> —June

Does she have a sense of humor?

Is she in good health?

Does she love her husband and treat him with kindness and respect?

Is she an equal partner with Your Beloved's dad in their marriage?

Do you have any shared interests?

Do you like her?

Can you tell if she likes you?

Your Beloved has been shaped by family experiences. To understand Your Beloved, it is vitally important to spend as much time as possible with your future in-laws. Remember, these are the folks who raised Your Beloved! This family will become your own. And as Your Beloved grows older and life experiences happen, Your Beloved will become more like his or her parents.

MARRIAGE WORKS!

Chapter 13

Mama's Girl? Daddy's Girl?

Mirror, mirror on the wall, I've become my mother after all.
—(Slogan on T-Shirt)

Grooms, look at your future mother-in-law carefully.

Spend time with her alone.
Does she remind you of Your Beloved?
Are there similar mannerisms or patterns of speech?
Is she athletic and attractive?
Is she healthy?
Does she work outside the home?
Does she keep up on current events and enjoy reading?
Is she a good cook?
Is she warm and loving, a care-giver?
Ask her questions about being a wife and mother.
Ask her questions about Your Beloved.
Does she speak about Your Beloved proudly?
Does she have a sense of humor?
Does she love Your Beloved's dad and treat him with kindness and respect?
Do you like her?
Can you tell if she likes you?

Grooms, look at your future father-in-law carefully.

Spend time with him alone. Perhaps without realizing it, Your Beloved will compare you to him. After all, he is her model of a husband and father.

Is he a good provider?

Is he an attentive and loving father?

Is he happily married to his wife?

Ask him questions about Your Beloved.

Does he speak about Your Beloved proudly?

Does he have a sense of humor?

Does he treat Your Beloved's mom with kindness and respect?

Do you have any shared interests?

Do you like him?

Can you tell if he likes you?

> Her dad said, "Welcome to the family, son. You must be the one. She has never brought anyone else home."
>
> —Conrad

> On a visit to her parents, I brought some military C-rations for my fiancée to try. Her dad looked worried, "Certainly hope you plan to provide better than this for my daughter!"
>
> —Fred

Be sure to meet Your Beloved's parents before you marry. Spend as much time as possible with them, both in their home and in your own. Many brides and grooms meet their in-laws for the first time at their wedding. Do not do this! These people hold the key to Your Beloved's behavior and expectations.

If it is apparent that the parents do not approve of you, how do you plan to resolve this problem? An on-going conflict with the in-laws is very stressful, will ruin many joyous occasions, and can undermine your marriage. Enlist Your Beloved's help in finding ways to improve this relationship before you marry.

Although "in-laws" are often listed as one of the three main problems faced by newlyweds (the others are sex and money), it is possible to have a warm, nurturing relationship with Your Beloved's parents. Begin now to work on this relationship. If however, you are unable or unwilling to do this, this is not your best choice!

Chapter 14

Your Future In-Laws

Does Your Beloved speak of his or her parents negatively, with hostility or hurt? Why?

Will this animosity affect your relationship with them or your relationship with each other?

Is there any desire to improve this relationship?

Have you spent a lot of time with your in-laws on many occasions? Have you spent enough time with them so that you are no longer nervous when you are with them?

Have you ever taken a vacation with them?

Have you spent several special holidays (birthdays, Christmas, Passover, Kwanzaa) with them?

Have you spent time with them when Your Beloved wasn't with you?

> I met my in-laws an hour before my wedding. I hated them! Her dad was pompous and overbearing, a real jerk. And her mom, what a bitch! They both got roaring drunk at the reception.
>
> —George

The first time I met my father-in-law, he spent hours criticizing his son. "Why would a smart gal like you want to marry a loser? He has always been a jerk. Why, in high school..."

—Helen

My mother-in-law was so opposed to the wedding that she insisted that the entire family not attend.

—Kim

My mother-in-law and I are best friends. She lends me clothes, buys me "no reason at all" presents, brings dinner every Sunday night (enough for an army), doggy sits and compliments me every chance she gets!

—LaVern

Take a picture of yourself with your in-laws and Your Beloved. This is your second family.

Do you fit into this picture?

If you look out of place, what would you have to give up or change in order to fit in?

Are you willing to do this?

My hair was waist length, my legs and underarms unshaved, no make up, long flowing skirts and sandals. His family was conservative, very formal, suits and ties, nylons, silk dresses, make up and permed hair. I looked at the photo and laughed until I cried.

—Skye

He is African American and I am Caucasian. Even our color photos were black and white.

—Tomi

When they took family photos, I was asked to step aside. The reason? I wasn't "family"!

—Donna

Have Your Beloved's parents done or said anything to you that made you uncomfortable?

Did you discuss this with Your Beloved?

I was his second wife. My in-laws were upset by the divorce and treated me like a home wrecker. I had no relationship with my mother-in-law until my son (their first grandchild) was born. Then all was forgiven.

—Karen

My in-laws refused to come to the wedding so I met them six months later. My mother-in-law was very cold to me, accused me of marrying her favorite son and taking him away from her. She told my husband, "Well, I guess she seems nice enough."

—Kathy

We were so young (19). We ran away and got married because we knew our parents wouldn't approve. When we talked to his mother, she set the tone for the next thirty-five years, "Oh Sara, I have always considered you one of my own!"

—Sara

Do you look forward to visiting with your future in-laws?
If you don't enjoy these visits, why not?
How often will visits be expected after you are married?

Will Your Beloved visit his parents without you?
How often do you plan to visit your own parents?
Will you visit without Your Beloved?

Visiting his parents every week was always an ordeal; finally I told him to take the twins and go without me. I couldn't handle the stress.

—Sheila

Every Christmas we fly to his parents' home for the holidays. Every summer we fly to the Cape for two weeks at the beach in the family cottage. I never imagined that all my vacation time would be spent with them.

—Annette

After convincing them I was sick, I'd send them all to my in-laws and then I'd spend the day pampering myself: soak in the tub, read magazines, nap. It was bliss!

—Missy

Have you eaten with them at their home?

Is their home more formal or less formal than your own?

> Dinner was always eaten in the dining room at 6:00 p.m. Father always wore his suit jacket, tie, and dress shirt to dinner. The table was set with bread and butter plates, salad plates, dessert plates and all the proper spoons, forks and knives. Conversation was lively, current events, history, politics and family lore. It was a special time.
>
> —Daniel

> Dinner was always eaten on the run: microwave dinners, take out food, sandwiches or bowls of cereal. We did sit down together for holiday meals.
>
> —Marian

> The white living room couches and chairs were covered with plastic. And the seat covers had sheets on top of them. I was never allowed in the living room; that was reserved for company.
>
> —Earl

> Her relationship with her folks was very reserved. It was "Yes, Sir" and "Yes, M'am." She was amazed that I called my parents "Ted" and "Alice."
>
> —Sidney

> Her mom had knick-knacks of pigs and little country pictures, gingham seat cushions and sunflowers all over the house. It was a shock! I grew up with modern art, leather couches, sconces and entertainment centers.
>
> —Thomas

Is Your Beloved close to his or her parents?

Are the parents consulted on an hourly, daily, or weekly basis before Your Beloved makes any decision?

Do your in-laws call frequently or visit without invitation?

Are you concerned that very personal information about you is discussed?

Is there room for you and your opinions in this relationship?

Do you expect this to change after you get married? Why?

Are the in-laws free with advice, opinions, information, money, gifts?

Do Your Beloved's parents say, "Well, we always do it this way."

Are they upset if you don't accept their advice or financial help?

Are you able to listen graciously, discuss their suggestions with Your Beloved, and then make your own decisions?

> When my parents got married they bought a house full of furniture, but it was years before they owned a car. When we got married, we didn't own any furniture but we did buy a new car. My parents were appalled.
>
> —Judy

> My parents were Depression survivors. They always paid cash for everything, or they didn't buy it. They insisted that we were headed for financial ruin because we used credit cards.
>
> —Ed

> My parents produced six babies, one every two years from the day they were married. We waited twelve years before we had children. Their comments never changed. "So when are you going to settle down and have children?"
>
> —Jessica

Will your in-laws live in the same city as you do once you're married? In the same house?

> My father-in-law gave us a house for our wedding present. The only hitch? It was right next door to the Family Home!
>
> —Wayne

> After the wedding, I moved into my husband's home, a block from his mother's. His mother had a key to his home and often walked in unexpectedly! Asking for the key back or changing the locks weren't options. "That would hurt her feelings!"
>
> —Louise

As newlyweds, we lived hundreds of miles from both parents. We learned to blend our family histories without interference!

—Marjorie

We moved in with his parents until we both finished college. They were really nice and supportive but I couldn't wait until we graduated and could have our own place. If I had it to do over, I'd wait to get married until we finished school.

—Jonnie

Are either of your in-laws alcoholics or drug users or compulsive gamblers?

Has Your Beloved attended support groups or received counseling to handle these problems?

Have you discussed how this may affect your relationship with each other or with them?

Both his parents were alcoholics. Both my parents were alcoholics. When we were dating, we mixed whiskey sours and washed our cars together.

—Muffy

I never brought my friends home. I never knew what I would find when I came home. I decided that I would never allow alcohol in my home.

—Ben

I should have known better. I worked with cocaine addicts. All the signs were there: poor health, chronic unemployment, erratic behavior. I just refused to see them.

—Jane

He told me stories about his dad's gambling, how the TV or the stereo were usually at the pawn shop, how there was only soup to eat at the end of the month, how his mom worked cleaning houses, and how he always had jobs to help out.

—Ruth

Was your mother-in-law or father-in-law unfaithful?

Were your parents unfaithful?

Patterns of behavior are learned in the family home. It isn't uncommon for a philandering father or mother to have philandering sons or daughters. If newspaper accounts are to be believed, the Kennedy family and numerous Hollywood stars are examples.

How will this affect your relationship with each other or with them?

> Her father had many mistresses. Although I was hardworking and faithful, she grilled me constantly. "Where were you? Where have you been? Were you out with other women? I can't trust you. I know you lie."
>
> —Cal

> He told me I was the only one. But he had affairs while we were engaged and this continued after we were married. It wasn't until much later that I learned his father did the same thing to his mother.
>
> —Marilyn

> My mom left with her lover when I was eight. I raised my younger brother and sisters. It was really tough. I want better for my kids.
>
> —Bruce

> After years of indifference and verbal abuse, his mother ran off with his father's best friend.
>
> —Peggie

In a conflict with your future in-laws, will Your Beloved support you, or side with them, or refuse to become involved?

Have Your Beloved's loyalties shifted from his or her family to you?

> My husband never allowed his family to be unkind to me. Once he even returned his house key and decided to cut all ties to his family until they apologized. They did too!
>
> —Leslie

> My in-laws are very critical. They make snide comments all the time. My husband either never hears them or says that I am too sensitive. If I get mad and say something, he demands that I apologize right away.
>
> —Mildred

Even if your future in-laws are cold, difficult, or unpleasant, will you be able to achieve a working relationship with them?

> You know, it's been thirty years and I still call my mother-in-law, "Mrs. Smith," or now that we have kids, "Grandma."
>
> —Mark

> I don't know how she does it, but she always knows when we are having a few relaxing moments; then she calls and riles everyone up!
>
> —Hanna

> After thirty-five years, my husband has less patience with his mother than I do. He finally sees just how manipulative she is!
>
> —Jesse

> Years ago my father-in-law had too much to drink and told me, "If I were picking daughter-in-laws, I wouldn't have picked you." The next day he called to apologize and I told him not to bother, I appreciated his honesty!
>
> —Arlene

> I am the only female in our home and after twenty-eight years of marriage, my mother-in-law still asks, "Who's this?" when I answer the phone!
>
> —Beverly

> When I answer the phone, my mother-in-law says, "Oh, it's you!" My husband bought me Caller ID so she won't ruin my day.
>
> —Diane

> "My husband is just like his dad, wonderful!"
>
> —Megan

> I am a mother-in-law and believe me, it's hard work. Little that I do or say is ever appreciated!
>
> —Willa

Getting along with your in-laws may require all the patience and love that you can muster. They will be your second family. Over the years, you will spend numerous special occasions with them.

And as they age, you may be called upon to take care of them or to settle their estate. Remember, you cherish their child, Your Beloved. If they never do another positive thing for you, they have given you a life mate!

MARRIAGE WORKS!

Chapter 15

Ethnic or Cultural Diversity

Is Your Beloved from a different ethnic or cultural background than you?

How will this affect your marriage?

1.
2.
3.
4.
5.

Do your parents and Your Beloved's parents support you and your marriage?

If they do not support you, have you discussed your plans to marry with them and listened to their concerns?

Do you agree or disagree with the issues raised by your future in-laws?

Will ethnic or cultural problems increase or decrease with time?

> Neither her parents nor my parents supported the marriage. After days of tears, shouting and arguments, everyone agreed to attend the wedding ceremony. We recently celebrated our fortieth wedding anniversary.
>
> —Ron

> My in-laws are racist! They didn't want their black son to marry a white woman. They never will accept me.
>
> —Meredith

> He was an orthodox Jew; I was a Gentile. The day we were married by the judge, they symbolically buried him.
>
> —MJ

> I met her over the Internet. She spoke Russian, but little English. I spoke no Russian. We met for a few days in Paris. It took months to straighten out all the papers, but finally we were married. After bringing her to the U.S., we are having real problems: she hasn't learned English, and I am sleeping on the couch.
>
> —Jeb

Do your siblings and friends support you and your marriage? If they do not support you, have you considered their concerns?

> I didn't listen to my friends and relatives. She was too young. She didn't speak much English. I didn't speak much Spanish. She thought I was very wealthy and that she would have servants. She wanted to live in the U.S. She didn't want to work or to have children. She just wanted to shop!
>
> —Tim

Have you discussed the community's response to an ethnically or culturally mixed marriage?

> I am a Jew, raised in Israel and I am seriously dating an Arab raised in Yemen. If we marry, we can't live in either of our homelands!
>
> —Simon

Will you and Your Beloved—or your children—be discriminated against because of this marriage?

Have you discussed what types of discrimination you might expect?

Are you willing to incorporate this cultural diversity into your marriage?

Do you speak Your Beloved's native language?

If not, will you learn this language?

Does Your Beloved speak your language?

Will you travel to Your Beloved's country to meet his or her family and friends?

Will your children learn to speak Your Beloved's native language?

Will you cook and serve ethnic foods in your home?

Will you change your style of dress if custom requires it?

Are women treated as less than equals in Your Beloved's country? Will Your Beloved treat you according to his cultural expectations?

Will you celebrate ethnic holidays?

> The girls learned to speak Chinese, to watercolor and to paint Chinese figures. They heard all the Chinese fairy tales and loved homemade Chinese food. They were taught to take the best from both cultures.
>
> —Leonard

> I absolutely refused to make tortillas from scratch! But I did cook pots and pots of beans. No matter how hard I tried, my Mexican dishes were never as good as his Mom's.
>
> —Jill

> It was hard for me to become Americanized. I didn't have any friends. I was very lonely. I lived for the times when my relatives visited. He said he would come home for lunch to keep me company but that would have made more work for me.
>
> —Ingrid

> Women are really second class citizens! At meals, I serve him and all his male relatives first. Standing in the kitchen, I eat whatever is left. Women are never allowed to give

their opinions and never consulted when decisions are made. Now our son and daughter are being raised the same way.

—Dottie

Ethnic or cultural diversity adds another dimension to a relationship. While your family, friends, and neighbors may not be as concerned with ethnic or cultural differences as they were in the past, you (or your children) will meet some people who are prejudiced.

Lack of support from your family and friends will definitely make this relationship with Your Beloved more difficult. Realistically discuss these issues.

You must be strongly committed to this relationship and to each other, to make this marriage work!

Chapter 16

Plans for a Child?

Do you want children?

Does Your Beloved want children?

Why or why not?

I never wanted a child but she insisted. I resented all the time he took and was relieved when he finally grew up and left home.

—Larry

I always wanted children; I even had their names picked out.

—Phil

We both wanted a large family and God blessed us with four healthy children.

—Aimee

She was a doctor and thought children would interfere with her career. She finally agreed to have children if I cut back on my hours and if I were the primary care-giver.

—Al

How many children do you or Your Beloved want?

When do you want these children?

Will you wait several years after you're married? Or do you plan to have a child immediately?

If your baby appears "off schedule," will this be a problem?

> We waited thirteen years before we had a baby; first the military and the Viet Nam War, then law school, then moving, starting new jobs, and paying back debts. Finally, we had time for a baby. My folks were so surprised that they asked, "Was this a mistake?"
>
> —James

> We had two children in the first two years we were married! I put him through college, but I had to drop out of school and I never have finished.
>
> —Blanche

Are either your parents or your in-laws pressuring you to have children?

> We had four babies immediately because he wanted to please his mother; she loved babies.
>
> —Lynn

> Every time I see them I ask them when am I going to be a grandma?
>
> —Grace

What did your parents do with you that you won't do with your own children? Discuss this with Your Beloved.

> His mother was super-critical with him. So he was super critical with our two children. Nothing they did was ever good enough. He undermined their self-esteem.
>
> —Denise

> They called me "The Mistake." I was tolerated! My two older brothers were put through college and are still helped financially. I worked my way through college.
>
> —Charles

> She hovered and waited on him hand and foot. She turned down his bed covers at night, cooked only his favorite foods, praised his every effort, never asked him to do anything around the house and spoiled him rotten.
>
> —Edna

What did your parents do with you that you will do with your own children?

Can you imagine Your Beloved as the nurturing parent of your child?

What characteristics does Your Beloved have that will make him or her a good parent? List them.

1.
2.
3.

Does Your Beloved have any characteristics that will make him or her a bad parent? Would you refuse to have children because of these characteristics? List them.

1.
2.
3.

> I always wanted children but with a full time job and a husband who is high maintenance, there is no way I can do it.
>
> —Kelly

Have you seen pictures of Your Beloved as a baby/child?

Can you imagine your child looking a bit like you and a lot like Your Beloved?

It amazes me that couples get married without discussing whether their marriage will include children. Believe it or not, some people don't like children and some career-minded people do not want children, ever! If you and Your Beloved can not agree on this issue, do not expect to win him or her over later. Do not half-heartedly agree just to end the discussion. Do not plan to trick him or her with a surprise pregnancy. If you cannot agree on this decision, Your Beloved is not your best choice.

MARRIAGE WORKS!

Chapter 17

Raising Your Child

Do you plan to continue working while you are pregnant?

Do you plan to return to work after the baby is born?

How many weeks of maternity leave do you plan to take?

Or do you plan to quit your job and stay home with the baby?

Were you/Your Beloved raised by a career mom who worked outside the home or a stay at home mom?

If you were raised in day care or by a nanny or relative, how do you feel about it?

Do you want this care for your child?

Were you ever mistreated?

Did you feel treasured, challenged, sad, abandoned or neglected? If you both plan to work after the birth of your child, do you both support this decision?

Who will take care of the baby? Live in nanny? Relative? Day care?

How many hours a day will you/Your Beloved be away from the child?

How much will child care cost?

After adding transportation, work clothes, and child care costs, will there be enough remaining from your salary to make this financially worthwhile?

If you both work after the birth of your child, who will stay home when the child is sick?

Who will take care of the child if you must work late or travel? Do you both agree that one of your careers is more important than the other?

If not, will you share the interruptions to your work day?

Do you/Your Beloved have a job that will allow you to take the child to work with you?

> After the babies, I began working part time. He works long hours with little flexibility. I take them to day care and school. I also take them to all medical appointments and leave work to take care of them when they are sick.
>
> —Lilly

Do you/Your Beloved have your own business or work from the home? Will one of you work days and the other nights, so that a parent is always home with the child?

Will you job share or work part-time in order to spend more time with the baby?

If you wish to stay home with your baby, does Your Beloved support this decision?

Will any of these arrangements decrease the amount of money you or Your Beloved makes?

What financial changes will have to be made, if any?

Although you both want children, have either of you had surgery to make this impossible (tubes tied or vasectomy)?

Is this procedure reversible?

Have you had discussions with a medical doctor to determine what is necessary to reverse this procedure?

> When I married him, he assured me that he wanted children. He said he would have his vasectomy reversed. He already had two children from his first marriage who visited regularly but lived with their mom. I love his children but I would like children of my own. Now he says two are enough.
>
> —Lee

What if you are unable to have a child?

Will you consider in-vitro fertilization or other modern medical techniques to become pregnant?

Will you consider a birth mother?

Will you consider adoption?

Will you be able to finance these procedures?

After testing, I learned that I couldn't have children. We immediately put our name in for adoption and now have three beautiful children, a girl and two boys.

—Connie

How many years do you want between your children?

What will you do if a "mistake" occurs?

Would you consider an abortion?

I had two children in two years. When I found out I was pregnant with the third, I sat down and cried. The doctor convinced me my health was in danger so I had an abortion. I still think about that baby; it would have been ten years old this year.

—Marian

I was forty years old and pregnant. My husband was furious and didn't speak to me for months.

—Carole

Do you plan to have an amniocentesis to determine the health or sex of your child?

If the test concludes that the child is spina bifida or Down Syndrome, will you consider an abortion?

If you determine not to have an abortion, are you prepared to raise a disabled child?

I was thirty-six when I became pregnant. My doctor urged me to have an amniocentesis to determine the health of the baby. I refused. I knew I wouldn't have an abortion, so why did I need the test? My doctor was furious with me!

—Miriam

Do you or Your Beloved feel you have to have a boy?

If it is a girl, will you consider an abortion?

> Without the benefit of an amniocentesis, the doctors still assured us that we were having a large healthy boy. I wasn't allowed in the delivery room. When the babies were born, the nurse announced, "Mr. Henry, two girls!" I couldn't believe it.
>
> —Jeff

Will you have to buy a larger car or move to a larger home? Or give up the family pet?

Have you discussed how having a child will change your relationship with each other: time together, finances, sex?

Are you/Your Beloved prepared to do everything necessary to have a healthy baby? This includes a good diet, exercise, no alcohol, cigarettes or drugs during pregnancy.

Do you plan to have a natural childbirth and to breast-feed the baby?

> I planned on the Earth Mother approach. No pain killers. The baby was breech and so I had a C-section. I was convinced that I was a failure.
>
> —Abigail

> He expected me to breast-feed my children because his mother did, but it really didn't appeal to me. It wasn't in style then and when I tried, it didn't feel good and I didn't have enough milk.
>
> —Ellen

Do either of you have experience taking care of a baby?
Did either of you take care of little brothers and sisters?
Did either of you baby-sit to earn money?

> I was an only child. I walked dogs and mowed lawns. I didn't know anything about babies.
>
> —Nina

Have you seen Your Beloved with infants or children?

Be sure to sit for a friend's baby to see Your Beloved's care and enjoyment of an infant and toddler. Plan events with a child and a teenager to see Your Beloved's attitude and enjoyment.

Is Your Beloved uncomfortable, short-tempered, anxious, delighted, loving, patient?

> On our first date, a little girl walked over to him and patted his arm. She wanted to try on his motorcycle helmet. He was so gentle with her. When he put his helmet on her head, she squealed with delight.
>
> —Leila

Have you discussed child-rearing philosophies with Your Beloved?

> I was stunned. Our attitudes are so different. She is anxious, hovers and meets every frivolous demand. She tolerates shrieking and whining. She is too attentive, too wrapped up in the girls. I don't exist.
>
> —Tony

Discuss the following questions with Your Beloved:

How would you/Your Beloved discipline your child?

Are "time outs" or "swats" or both acceptable?

How would you/Your Beloved deny your child an item he or she wants?

Would either of you give in to whining or a temper tantrum, especially on the floor of a large busy store?

> He constantly undermined my efforts at discipline. He would "ride in" like some white knight and save the child from punishment. She never was held responsible for any misbehavior.
>
> —Lorie

If the baby is hungry, will you feed on demand or rigidly adhere to a schedule allowing the baby to cry for 30 minutes or more in order to maintain the schedule?

> The baby sat in his seat on top of the table and screamed the entire time his mom ate dinner. "I'm hungry. I'm not going to stop eating just to feed him. He'll have to wait."
>
> —Laura

How would you/Your Beloved help your child overcome a fear, for example, fear of the dark or fear of dogs?

Our little boy was afraid of the dark so I put a night light in his room. His dad laughed at him for needing a light and called him "sissy pants."

—Esther

Our little girl was afraid to go to sleep. Every night he made up stories and sang songs until she became sleepy. She would snuggle against him, sigh and yawn. He put kisses into her hands to hold onto while she slept.

—Alicia

Do you/Your Beloved believe that your child should have chores? If so, what chores?

Should your child have an allowance or a job?

I always had chores; the usual stuff: take out the garbage, clean up my room, do the dishes. But she never had chores. Her mother never even let her in the kitchen.

—Andy

Do you expect your child to have his or her own room, telephone, television set, stereo, computer, Internet connection?

Do you plan to give your sixteen-year-old a car? Why?

Do you want your child to go to college?

Their child was a few weeks old when a large glass bottle filled with dimes and quarters appeared on the counter of their restaurant. There was a picture of their infant and a note, "Send Amy to college."

—Nancy

Do you plan to start a savings account for your child now?

Do you or Your Beloved support the idea of "quality time" (a few short special minutes a day with your child) or "quantity time" (most or all of the day with your child)?

Within days of the birth of her second child, she was working ten-hour days, taking work home and traveling. The baby walked and spoke her first words with the nanny. Quality time? "I try to take her to the doctor if she is sick."

—Steffie

You can't schedule quality time. Sometimes a flash of quality appears in quantity time.

—Marty

Some day care center isn't raising my kids! I am.

—Jennifer

Do you/Your Beloved plan to raise your child in a religion?
Will your child be baptized?
Is there a family christening dress the child will wear?
Will you invite the grandparents to the ceremony?

His parents were indifferent Christians. Their Catholic nanny was horrified when she learned that the child was never baptized. She immediately took him to church to be baptized.

—Teddy

Our sons wore the christening dress I had worn. The grandparents were there and many of the relatives. Our best friends stood up with us as the godparents. It was a very special time.

—Peter

Children: when to have them and how to raise them and their impact on your lives will demand a great deal of your time and attention. "Let's see, four boys, two years apart, named Aaron, Cooper, Thatcher, and Jason, swimming and baseball, and of course college."

Now that's planning! Discuss these issues in general now. Compare your childhood and Your Beloved's. Discuss how your children's family life will differ from your own. And remember, that delightful tow-headed child will grow up into a delightful tow-headed teenager and eventually a delightful tow-headed adult. You, however, will always remain the parent!

MARRIAGE WORKS!

Chapter 18

Money, Money, Money

Will there be financial equality in your home?

> My grandpa refused to give my grandma 5 cents to buy a spool of thread to mend his socks. She was over the budget!
>
> —Leila

Will you or Your Beloved control the money?

Will spending and saving questions be decided jointly?

Is money a power issue with you or Your Beloved?

Who will write the checks to pay the monthly bills?

Will any bills be directly deducted from your/Your Beloved's paycheck?

Who will balance the checkbook?

Who will figure out and file the income taxes?

Have you discussed these issues and are you both comfortable with these arrangements?

My husband was stunned to learn that I never balanced my checkbook and didn't have any idea how much money was in my account. When my checks bounced, he was horrified!

—Denise

My dad made all the money and all the money decisions. My mom ran our household on a weekly allowance. I refuse to spend my adult life on an allowance.

—Cora

He was appalled at my lack of money sense. I had always had plenty of money to buy anything I wanted. I had never budgeted in my life.

—Eve

I didn't plan on a career. I wanted to be a customer.

—Frances

I don't know how she does it. She can squeeze pennies out of a rock. I just turn my paycheck over to her. The bills are always paid on time and our savings account keeps growing.

—Greg

How compatible are you and Your Beloved on the issue of money?

Do you or Your Beloved own numerous articles of clothing that have never been worn, new books that have never been read, tapes and CDs still in their cellophane wrapper?

Do you or Your Beloved still wear a high school jacket (20 years later), eat cold meat "ends," and cut down your Dad's suits and ties for work?

How would you describe your spending/saving personality? Your Beloved's? Circle the words that fit:

Spendthrift? Impulsive Buyer? Frugal? Cheap? Cautious?

Bargain Hunter? Garage Sale Addict? Coupon Clipper?

Compulsive Shopper? Miser?

How much money do you/Your Beloved need to be happy per week? $________ month? $________ year? $________

How much money is enough money? $__________

If you won $1,000,000.00, how would you spend it?
How would Your Beloved spend it?
Would you or Your Beloved save any? How much?
Do you believe that you should save and then buy?
Or buy and pay for it later?
Are there certain items that you would always pay in cash or always charge?
What is Your Beloved's point of view? Do you agree?
If not, how do you plan to resolve this issue?

We always saved our money until we could afford a vacation or a new car. We never borrowed money for either of these items.

—Jack

We used credit cards for everything. We spent it before we made it. Our salaries just bought down the credit card debt.

—Kate

He complained constantly about a large jar of "bargain" jam that tasted awful and ruined his morning toast. He figured that it would take six months (eating it every day) to finish the jar. I suggested that he throw the jam away. He was horrified!

—Lillian

In the three years that we knew them, they had purchased two different sets of living room and dining room furniture, changed the draperies, and purchased a boat, a truck, two cars, hunting equipment, skis and ...

—Matt

I was thousands of dollars in debt. I never paid cash for anything. I had a line of credit with the bank. Whenever a client paid, the money went to the bank to pay down the debt.

—Scott

> On vacation, she spent more than $300.00 for T-shirts to be given to her friends as gifts. Then she decided that she liked them all and kept them. All of them!
>
> —Frank

> She came from a very wealthy family. As an associate in the firm, I knew I would never be able to offer her the lifestyle to which she was accustomed.
>
> —Robert

Do you have a checking account? A savings account? Credit cards? Does Your Beloved?

Do you/Your Beloved balance your checkbooks every month?

What items do you/Your Beloved usually charge on a credit card?

Do you/Your Beloved pay off the credit card balances every month?

Do either of you owe more than $500.00 to a credit card company?

Do either of you gamble? If so, how often? What are your monthly losses?

Is one of you a compulsive gambler?

> My husband was a compulsive gambler. Money just disappeared. I've had the sheriff at the door. The utilities cut off. I've been evicted for not paying the rent. I've been forced to declare bankruptcy.
>
> —Sandy

Have either of you borrowed money from your parents?

How much is owed?

Are you expected to pay this money back?

Or are you/Your Beloved's parents standing by to give you more money when needed?

Do either of you have college loans? How much is still owed? $________________

Are either of you obligated to pay alimony or child support?

What will be your combined annual income? $______________

Yours? $______________

Your Beloved's? $______________

What will be your combined debt? $______________

Yours? $______________

Your Beloved's? ______________

Will you both continue to work outside the home after your marriage?

Do either of you have plans to quit work? Change your jobs? Go back to school? Stay home with children?

Are either of your companies "downsizing"?

Are either of you in danger of losing your jobs?

If either of you loses your job or stops working, will you be able to meet all your financial obligations?

What emergency plans do you have to meet this situation?

Are either of you in line for a promotion?

Money, who makes it, who spends it, and for what, are hotly contested issues. Finances are one of the primary problem areas in many marriages. It is a sensitive topic rarely discussed before marriage.

Differences in your spending and saving styles must be discussed before you marry; such issues as a budget, debts, and joint checking/savings accounts or credit cards must be faced. While it is difficult for a spendthrift and a miser to communicate financially, it can be done!

MARRIAGE WORKS!

Chapter 19

For Richer or For Poorer

List your/Your Beloved's assets:

Property
Stocks and Bonds
Savings Accounts
Checking Accounts
Trust/Alimony/Child Support Payments
Anything else?

List your/Your Beloved's debts or monthly obligations:

Mortgage payments/Rent
Loans
Car payments
Credit card payments
Alimony or child support payments
Insurance
Utilities
Food
Savings
Planned Purchases - wedding expenses, new car, house
What else?

Have you set up joint checking and savings accounts?

Do you have joint credit cards?

If not, do you plan to do this once you are married?

Or will you continue your individual checking, savings accounts, and credit card accounts?

If you do maintain separate accounts, have you discussed who will pay for what?

What expenses will be shared? And what expenses will you pay for alone?

How much will be set aside monthly for personal use or savings?

> We maintain separate accounts but share all our expenses 50-50, including alcohol which I don't drink and cigarettes which he doesn't smoke, steak, which I don't eat, and yogurt, which he doesn't eat. He out-earns me by $40,000 per year and graciously allowed me to pay him back without interest for the expensive vacation we took that I couldn't afford!
>
> —Vivian

> We didn't have much but we put what we had together. There wasn't his money and my money; there was only our money!
>
> —Wendy

Are either of you quite wealthy?

Have either of you filed for bankruptcy?

Are either of you expecting to receive an inheritance? Are there any restrictions on the use of this inheritance?

Have you/Your Beloved discussed any plans for this inheritance? If you disagree on the use of these monies, how will this be resolved?

> My family was quite wealthy. And I made substantially more money at my job than he did. This was a constant source of irritation.
>
> —Annie

> My trust fund matures when I am 26. I toyed with the idea of a year off, round the world trip but I knew that a down

> payment on property was a more practical use of the money. But I don't want her making my decision for me!
>
> —Bennett

Do you and Your Beloved have medical or dental health insurance? Property insurance? Life insurance?

Who is the beneficiary on these policies?

If you are not currently the beneficiary, will this be changed once you are married?

> His mom was listed as the beneficiary on all his policies. He didn't plan to change that but he told me if we had any children, he would list them as beneficiaries.
>
> —Carla

> He immediately changed all his policies to list me as a beneficiary. I felt very cared for and loved.
>
> —Delia

Equally worthy of discussion is the issue of savings.

Do you have a savings account? Does Your Beloved?

How much money is in these savings accounts?

Yours? $____________________

Your Beloved's? $____________________

Do you plan to combine all your assets?

Do you and Your Beloved have a savings plan?

What percentage of your earnings do you plan to save?

Are you saving for something in particular? A house? A new car? A luxury vacation?

Do you both agree on your savings priorities?

List your savings priorities here.

1.
2.
3.
4.
5.

Are there assets held by you or Your Beloved that will remain separate?

And if so, is either of you suggesting a prenuptial agreement restricting the distribution of certain assets if a divorce occurs?

If either partner wants a prenuptial agreement, it is imperative that these delicate discussions occur before you are sitting in the lawyer's office.

> This was my second marriage. I had a successful business and children from my first marriage. I wanted to protect them. So, I took her to the lawyer's office and he explained the papers. She was furious and stormed out of the office. She said I didn't trust her. But it wasn't a question of trust; it was a question of MONEY.
>
> —Fred

> This isn't easy. I mean, there is a real question of trust here. But I have a home, several cars, a vacation cottage, stocks and bonds... And what if I ask and she refuses to sign the papers? Then I'll begin to wonder, why won't she sign? Does she plan to split with my stuff? But if she does sign, she'll know that I don't trust her.
>
> —Jon

> This was my third marriage. I had a business and a house. I didn't feel right getting married without a prenuptial agreement. He didn't mind at all. He said, "I love you honey; I just want to spend the rest of my life with you! I'll sign anything you want."
>
> —Katherine

In a committed relationship between equal partners who willingly communicate, even the topic of assets and debts can be discussed.

If Your Beloved is unwilling to share financial information with you, ask why. If you are concerned about Your Beloved's financial history and the impact it will have on your married financial stability, Your Beloved may not be your best choice.

Chapter 20

Budget Your Money

Regardless of the amount of money you make a year, a budget will help to avoid arguments about money. But a budget will only be successful if you both support it.

Have you and Your Beloved written out a budget?

When we got married, we were starving newlyweds. We ate chicken pot pies (25 cents each) and Jell-O. We slept on the floor in sleeping bags and rode our bicycles when we couldn't afford gas for the car. There wasn't much money to budget, but we did anyway. We even had a "savings jar" of pennies.

—Phoebe

We always overspent under the first budget. We changed it constantly; first because of the new house, then because of the baby. Now we stop spending if our credit card debt exceeds $1,500.

—Rita

The budget was the hardest thing we ever did together! We couldn't agree on the amount for personal spending, for savings, or for food. He had college loan payments. I had credit card debt from being out of work. He had child support payments. It was a nightmare!

—Joey

She wanted $20,000 in savings in five years. Every discussion was about "can we afford it" or "you can't buy that." When we had friends over, they had to bring their own steaks to grill and their own beer. We provided the potatoes.

—Hank

Regardless of the amount of your joint income, write out your budget together. Sit down now, discuss each item, and commit to staying within the guidelines.

Once you have made the budget, do you agree that the amounts listed are realistic? What will you do if either or both of you consistently exceed the budget? Discuss the consequences.

Larry Burkett in *The Complete Financial Guide for Young Couples* has suggestions for a budget for You and Your Beloved.

Making your budget together

1. List and then total your monthly income (include salaries, alimony/child support payments, investment dividends, etc.):

You

Your Beloved

2. List and then total *all* your monthly expenses:

Mortgage payment or rent

Food

Utilities (electricity, gas, water, sewer, garbage, telephone, etc.)

Car payment

Insurance

Personal Allowances

Debt (credit cards, college loans, etc.)

Alimony/Child Support

Savings

Entertainment (cable television, alcohol, tobacco, sports tickets, health club membership, hobbies, vacations, etc.)

Medical and Dental Care

Taxes (State and Federal Income Taxes)

Miscellaneous

3. Subtract your monthly expenses from your monthly income. If expenses are greater than income, discuss how to limit your spending until your expenses are less than your income. If your income is greater than your expenses, discuss what to do with your savings.

MARRIAGE WORKS!

Chapter 21

Plan for Retirement—Now!

Do you both have retirement funds? Or IRAs? Or 401Ks?

What do you plan to do when you retire?
Scale back?
Move to a smaller home or apartment?
Buy a mobile home and travel?
Live on your pension?
Get a part-time job?
Move in with relatives?
Buy a boat and sail around the world?

Although this may be years away, it is always helpful to explore each other's retirement plans.

> I came home one day and there was a "For Sale" sign on my home. I asked my husband if we planned to move. "Yes," he said, "somewhere warmer than this"!
>
> —Kelly

> He loves golf and always wanted to live alongside a golf course. I can't play golf and have no desire to learn. I want a private yard not a putting green.
>
> —Lei

He never retired. At eighty-three, he still walks downtown and opens his office every day.

—Marty

I married him for better or for worse but not for lunch!

—Wise Old Saying

His dream was to live on a fishing boat when he retired. I can't swim, don't fish, and get land sick every time we dock. We sold our 5,000 square-foot house, bought a fishing boat and stay out in the ocean three weeks at a time. I left my father in a nursing home, my children, my church, my music and my friends.

—Edna

Has either of you considered an early retirement?

If so, how will this affect your finances?

What planning should be done now to allow an early retirement?

As my plumber handed me his bill, he told me that he planned to be sunbathing in Florida when he turned forty. He had two years to go!

—Hillary

He had his whole life planned out. First career military, then fly cargo planes, then own a bar in Hawaii. It all sounded great to me.

—Erica

Do you or Your Beloved have a Last Will and Testament?

Do you plan to change this Will once you are married?

Do you plan to leave assets to each other?

Will you make special bequests?

This is particularly important if this is a second marriage.

When he died without a Will, his second wife and his step-son took the house, cars, antique furniture, and oriental rugs. His adult children by his first wife inherited nothing.

—Martha

He died suddenly and unexpectedly after a brief illness. His Will left everything to his first wife.

—Harriet

It is never too early to discuss your golden retirement years, especially if you or Your Beloved have dreams that will drastically change your lifestyle. From corporate executive to beachcomber, from spacious mountain home to cramped fishing boat or house trailer, from metropolitan city to wide-open spaces, share these dreams with each other. If you can't support these lifestyle changes, begin looking for a compromise now!

MARRIAGE WORKS!

Chapter 22

Live to Work or Work to Live?

Do you work to live or live to work?

How many hours are you required to work each week?

How many hours do you actually work?

Do you always volunteer for overtime?

On a regular basis, do you bring work home in the evenings?

Do you work on the weekends?

Will the number of hours you work increase or decrease after you marry?

Do you consider yourself a workaholic? Does Your Beloved?

> He works long hours at the office and then brings home a briefcase full of work to do at home. His boss told him he has to work a minimum of sixty hours a week to keep his job!
>
> —Mary Ellen

> Before we owned the lodge, he worked such long hours plus commuting that the kids and I never saw him. Now we work together.
>
> —Molly

All her clients have our home number. Every night she spends hours on work-related calls.

—Al

Do you have sick leave and vacation leave? How many days per year?

In addition to your vacation days, do you have certain holidays off each year? Which holidays?

Are there certain holidays that you are expected to work?

Do you expect Your Beloved to work? For how long?

We had just bought a very expensive home based on both our paychecks. Within months of the purchase, my wife told me she was tired of working and quit her job.

—Andrew

If you both work, will you be able to schedule vacation leave at the same time?

How long have you held your current job?

I changed jobs when we got married. Now I work for him. I keep the books for him and do all the tax filings. I love working with him. What could be better? My best friend and life mate as my boss!

—Maggie

What training was necessary to qualify for your current job?

Is this training complete?

Are you expected to take additional courses in the future?

Do you enjoy your job? What do you like about it? What do you dislike about it?

Do you like or dislike your boss?

Does your boss like or dislike you?

Do you like or dislike your co-workers?

Do your co-workers like or dislike you?

Do you consider your job stressful? Why?

As minister to a large congregation, I never have an uninterrupted evening with my own family. Someone is always in crisis and needing help.

—Luke

The corporation had a spouses' function and the President of the company told us not to interfere with our spouses' careers. If we didn't support them working a seventy-hour workweek (including Saturdays) then the spouses should get another job.

—Sally

Is your job physically dangerous? Why?

Has your job negatively affected your health in the past year? What ailments do you believe are job related?

Have you considered quitting your current job? Why?

Are you currently interviewing for a new job?

If you get this new job, will it mean an increase in responsibility and salary or a move to another city?

Does Your Beloved support this change?

Does your job require rotating shifts or work at night?

I work the day shift and she works the night shift. We see each other every other weekend.

—Ed

Is your work seasonal?

What do you do on the "off season"?

Does your job require travel?

My husband travels more than 100,000 miles a year. Sometimes I feel like a single parent!

—Edie

He drives a truck and is gone for weeks at a time. The money is great but I sure do miss him! He can't find a job here at home.

—Meg

How often do you travel?

Will the amount you travel increase or decrease after you marry? Can Your Beloved accompany you when you travel?

Does your job require lengthy absences or unaccompanied overseas tours?

> He quit his 9 to 5-job here and took a job in Iran. I only saw him a few times during the seven years we were married.
>
> —Denise

> My husband is in the military. He is often gone for months on unaccompanied tours.
>
> —Linda

Will your job affect, change, or make new demands on Your Beloved's life?

> My husband is the minister of a large church. There is no question that his job impacts my life. I must dress conservatively, speak quietly, watch the deportment of our children, and participate in church functions by teaching Sunday school, singing in the choir, visiting shut-ins, arranging senior functions. I'm the unpaid "junior" minister. The congregation would not tolerate me having a career of my own.
>
> —PJ

> As a military officer's wife, I was told what to wear to certain "command" performances (gloves and a modest Sunday-type dress), to call on the general's wife as soon as we moved to the base, to attend all the ladies' afternoon teas, charity functions, and base activities and never to question the commander's opinions. If I acted improperly, it would harm my husband's career.
>
> —Sue

> My husband was a corporate executive. I was expected to entertain on a regular basis. None of the corporate wives had their own careers; their career was to further their husband's career! The company moved us every few years, which made it impossible for me to have a career of my own.
>
> —Helen

Reported in the *Rocky Mountain News,* Coach McCartney's wife, Lyndi McCartney says their thirty-five years of marriage was a "traditional 1950s marriage" in which "the wife reared the children and sacrificed herself while the husband pursued his career ambitions."

As a doctor, my wife worked long hours and was always on call when she wasn't at the hospital. I sacrificed my career to take care of the family. As househusband, I raised the kids, was the Homeroom Mom, and did the cooking and the cleaning.

—Samuel

How many jobs have you/Your Beloved held prior to this one?

Are you currently unemployed?

Have you ever been fired? Why?

Have you ever quit a job? Why?

Has either of you been unemployed for long periods of time? Why?

Has either of you ever been on welfare or received unemployment compensation or food stamps?

Is either of you opposed to receiving federal aid?

My husband hasn't worked in years! After he was squeezed out of his job at the bank, he tried to find work. He lost his next job when his company merged with a competitor. He tried working for himself but that failed too.

—Louise

When we got married, my husband was out of work. Now he is the househusband and we both love it.

—Roberta

I never wanted to be the breadwinner but my husband didn't make enough to support us. I worked long hours as a secretary and he stayed home, watched the soaps, and the kids.

—Agnes

When we married, she was a dedicated career woman. After out little girl was born, she fired five different nannies. She couldn't find a nanny who satisfied her. Finally, we both agreed that she should stay home.

—Jack

I work part-time now that we have kids. It really is the best of all worlds. I work while they are in school and I am home when they are home.

—Edna

Have you ever been injured at work?

How did this happen? Are you fully recovered?

Are work-related injuries possible at any time?

If you are injured at work, will your company cover your medical expenses and salary during the time you are recovering?

What are your career goals?

Is this the job you plan to have five, ten, or fifteen years from now?

If not, what do you plan to do instead?

First I taught elementary school. Then I graduated from law school and became a lawyer. Now I'm an author. My career continues to evolve.

—Larry

I always wanted to be a doctor, so after my military career I went back to school. Now I am an emergency room physician and I love it.

—Brad

I decided I would be president of my own company by the time I was thirty-five!

—Sonia

Every few years I change my career. I was a landscape architect, a city planner, a professor. And every time I change my career, I also change my wife!

—Carl

Do you plan to change careers?

Will you have to go back to school to change careers?

Will you quit your current job to attend school? Or will you attend night school and work your day job too?

Does Your Beloved support your desire for additional education that should lead to a higher-paying job?

My ex-husband was very unsupportive; every time I tried to better myself, I only got negative comments.

—Donna

When my husband was stationed overseas, he received a telegram from me saying that I would be sitting next to him in law school that fall. He was thrilled!

—Lara

I always wanted to be a marriage counselor. After my children were grown, I went back to school. My husband struggled with this for a long time. Now that I am graduated and have my own practice, he is very proud of me.

—Gail

I decided to go to law school. After years of study, working part-time and having my wife support me, I flunked the bar twice.

—John

My husband divorced me soon after I finished school. The effort to work and study really took its toll. I lost track of my kids and my husband. He found someone else.

—Jennifer

Do both you and Your Beloved work outside the home?

Do you both work nine to five?

Do either of you work shorter hours?

Who will arrive home first?

Will the one home first be responsible for additional household chores, shopping, laundry, dinner preparation?

Are your income levels similar or do one of you earn more than the other?

Is this likely to change in the future?

Do you mind that Your Beloved earns more than you do?

When we first started working, I made $2,000 more than my husband. He mentioned that to his boss and immediately got a raise. "Why, we can't have the little lady making more than you do!"

—Lydia

I always made more money than my husband. It was a continuing sore spot.

—Monica

She owns her own company; she owns the home we live in; why should I mind?

—Fred

Will your job require you to move to another city some day in the future?

Will Your Beloved support this move?

Will it be a problem to move away from your parents, friends, home?

Will it be difficult for Your Beloved to locate a job in this new city?

Will you have to move numerous times during your career?

If Your Beloved can't locate a new job or is unhappy about moving, will you refuse to move?

Will refusing to move limit your career opportunities?

I married a forest ranger. When he was stationed out west, I refused to leave my East Coast friends and my parents. We visited back and forth for awhile, but our long distance marriage ended in divorce.

—Dee

I was a career Navy officer. My wife was increasingly unhappy with the frequent moves and the unaccompanied overseas tours. Finally tired of her complaints, I retired from the Navy.

—Edgar

He was a company man. We moved every few years, from New England to California to London to Texas to Colorado. It was really an adventure to raise our children all over the world!

—Isabel

It's hard to move a two-career family. When he received an offer for a high-powered job out west, I agreed to leave my teaching job and move. It was the best decision for all of us.

—Kitty

Do you consider that one of your jobs is "more important" or "prestigious" than the other?

Does one of you have more flexibility (hours, leave, absences) than the other?

How will this affect you as a family?

> I was an accountant. She was a plastic surgeon. No question, her job was more prestigious!
>
> —Sidney

> I was the housewife. He was the physician. I tried to meet his every need. It was never enough.
>
> —Mildred

> We agreed on gender roles. I stayed home to care for the family and he worked to support us. We both believe that our contributions are equally valuable.
>
> —Jill

Has Your Beloved ever served in the military?

Did Your Beloved receive an honorable discharge?

If Your Beloved received a less than honorable discharge, ask for details!

Will this less than honorable discharge affect his ability to get a good job?

Will it affect your relationship in other ways?

Large portions of every day will be spent at work away from Your Beloved. Being able to discuss your workday with Your Beloved is one of the benefits of being in a committed relationship.

If Your Beloved is uninterested in your workday, if you are uninterested in Your Beloved's workday, both successes and failures, this person isn't your best choice!

MARRIAGE WORKS!

Chapter 23

Employment Record

Ask Your Beloved to fill out this employment record for the last three jobs held.

How long has Your Beloved held each job?

What are the reasons given for changing jobs?

Is there an obvious pattern of advancement or of unemployment?

Once you've done that, fill out the employment record with your own information and answer the same questions about yourself for Your Beloved.

EMPLOYMENT RECORD

Current or most recent job

Company Name ______________________________

Company Address ______________________________

Company Phone Number ______________________________

Name of Immediate Supervisor______________________________

Supervisor's Phone Number______________________________

Dates Employed ______________________________

Position Held ______________________________

Reason for Leaving______________________________

Previous job

Company Name ______________________________

Company Address ______________________________

Company Phone Number ______________________________

Name of Immediate Supervisor______________________________

Supervisor's Phone Number______________________________

Dates Employed ______________________________

Position Held ______________________________

Reason for Leaving______________________________

Previous job

Company Name ______________________________

Company Address ______________________________

Company Phone Number ______________________________

Name of Immediate Supervisor______________________________

Supervisor's Phone Number______________________________

Dates Employed ______________________________

Position Held ______________________________

Reason for Leaving______________________________

Chapter 24

Sex!

Marie was marrying a minister. They were not intimate before they married. All her friends were worried because she hadn't been able to "check out the goods".

—Angela

Two weeks before we were married, I was feeling sexy and tried to interest my fiancé. He was bored with the whole idea and admitted that I didn't turn him on.

—Mary

All he ever thinks about is SEX SEX SEX.

—Patti

He is the sweetest most considerate lover. I love making love to him!

—Sunny

His disease caused impotence. It's been nine years without sex. That was one of the few things we did together that I really enjoyed.

—Claire

If you are truly in love, sex waits until marriage!

—Mary and Jim

I was a virgin before I met him. Then I had sex with him on the first date. He laughed because I was so embarrassed and inexperienced. I admit, I didn't like it much. But he did. We were married a few weeks later.

—Daisy

I wore white at our wedding and so did my wife. We were both virgins. It was so special that we saved ourselves for each other.

—Cameron

Sex. Virginal and waiting for your wedding night?

Numerous premarital experiences prior to meeting Your Beloved?

Other affairs plus Your Beloved at the same time?

Too much? Not enough?

Abusive? Gentle and romantic?

Pornographic sex?

Cybersex?

This is a topic that must be discussed with Your Beloved. Are you committed to each other exclusively, to not having sexual affairs with anyone else?

I had an affair with a married man. He divorced his wife and married me. I was ecstatic. Then he had affairs when he was married to me. Why was I surprised?

—Bonnie

Is your relationship only a sexual one?

We were both divorced and became intimate immediately. I never met his family or friends but I did meet his dog. He invited me to his home only if mine weren't available. He ignored my birthday and Valentines Day and gave me a tacky second-hand Christmas present. And he continued to see his married pregnant mistress.

—Carole

> I'm sorry that I didn't wait. I got caught up in the male machismo bit. You know, sowing-wild-oats-prove-you're-a-man stuff.
>
> —Owen

> She was much more experienced than I was. It always made me uncomfortable. Was I doing it right?
>
> —Noah

> I just wanted sex. I didn't want a relationship.
>
> —Leo

> My little head told my big head what to do. What a mistake!
>
> —Hank

> I spent my honeymoon at the pharmacy getting a prescription filled for venereal disease. My husband had slept with a whore before we were married.
>
> —MarySue

Have you and Your Beloved decided to postpone an intimate relationship until after marriage?

If so, have you arrived at this decision through a religious conviction, fear of pregnancy, or other reasons?

> We had been physically intimate for months but the worry about an unplanned pregnancy created too much tension. Now we have decided to stop intimate sexual relations until after we are married.
>
> —Stan

> We waited until after we were married. Her parents would have killed me if we hadn't! It was hard but I'm really glad we did!
>
> —Jonathan

> My mom always told me, "Son, if you don't wait for your wedding night, you will be cheating yourself out of the best time of your life." I decided to wait.
>
> —Phil

If you are waiting for your wedding night, how do you plan to control any frustration you may experience prior to your wedding?

Are you and Your Beloved currently in an intimate relationship?

> Nice girls don't sleep around. So since I was having sex with him I felt that I had to marry him. Within a matter of months I knew I had made a big mistake. By then I was pregnant and it was too late.
>
> —Annette

> We were put in separate bedrooms when we visited his folks but I'm sure they knew we were intimate.
>
> —Bonnie

> I'm really sorry we didn't wait. Our honeymoon was just another weekend.
>
> —Jim

If you are sexually active, have you discussed and adopted a very conservative birth control method?

Is this birth control method used consistently? Are both of you responsible for using the birth control method?

If an unplanned pregnancy results, how will you and Your Beloved deal with this? Discuss this now!

Set a wedding date?
Move up the wedding date?
Single motherhood?
Abortion?
Adoption?
Will this end your relationship?

> He refused to accept any responsibility for the "slip." It was all my fault. He was convinced that I did it on purpose to get married. As soon as I told him, he packed up and moved out.
>
> —Judy

> We had to get married. Both of our parents were furious! We were very much in love and I know we would have married anyway but I keep telling my girls, "Don't have a baby until you've been married a few years!"
>
> —Elsa

> I knew he wouldn't have married me if I hadn't gotten pregnant. And yes, I got pregnant on purpose.
>
> —Esther

> Neither of us were in any position to raise a child. We put him up for adoption. It was the most difficult decision we have ever made.
>
> —Cara

> I was five months pregnant when I got married. The white wedding dress was way too tight! After the baby was born, we told everyone he was premature. A seven and one half pound preemie? I'm sure we didn't fool anyone.
>
> —Laura

> I never even discussed it with him. I just took time off from work for the abortion. It still bothers me. Was it a boy or a girl?
>
> —Lauren

Do you and Your Beloved enjoy physical closeness: hand holding, hugs, kisses, caresses?

Do you and Your Beloved enjoy cuddling, without the need for sexual intimacy?

Do you feel physically attracted to Your Beloved?
What does he or she do that excites you?
Have you discussed this with Your Beloved?

Do you have the same level of sexual desire as Your Beloved?

Have you refused to have sexual relations?
How did Your Beloved react to your refusal?

List five loving activities that you and Your Beloved particularly enjoy.

1.
2.
3.
4.
5.

Has Your Beloved ever suggested you do anything you found to be embarrassing, unpleasant, or hurtful?

How did Your Beloved react if you refused to do what was asked? Was Your Beloved angry, hurt, understanding?

After knowing how you feel, has Your Beloved ever asked again?

> He insisted that I have relations with his best friend. I didn't want to and begged him to stop asking me. Finally, I gave in and did it while he watched. Now he calls me "slut" and "whore."
>
> —Mary

Do you or Your Beloved use pornographic materials?

Have you discussed this?

How do you feel if Your Beloved plans to use pornographic materials after you are married?

Sex sells cars, mouthwash, blue jeans, and jewelry. Hollywood sells sex between two movie stars within the first ten minutes of the movie. Couples are bombarded with sexually suggestive reading material and programs. Regardless, a marriage based on sex alone will not last a lifetime.

Having sex on the first date or within the first months of dating is a very bad idea. A sexual relationship consumes your thoughts; it deludes you into thinking that this is your best choice. Couples who enter a sexual relationship before they become friends, before they determine if they are compatible, before they are committed to this relationship, before they have imminent plans to marry have entered into the zone of ultimate dating, but they have not entered into a committed relationship that will produce a lifetime marriage.

Chapter 25

Prior Sexual Encounters

Prior to this relationship, were you sexually active?

Was Your Beloved? Test your level of communication in this relationship by discussing this.

Have you asked Your Beloved how many lovers he or she had prior to your relationship?

What answers were you given?

> I found out later he was a player and had numerous women, including several when we were dating.
>
> —Lana

> He told me he had two other affairs before we met. He insisted I tell him how many I had had.
>
> —Julianne

> Why should I tell him? What I did before I met him is none of his business.
>
> —Ariel

Has Your Beloved asked you?

Do you trust and believe that Your Beloved will tell you the truth?

If Your Beloved is unwilling to tell you, how do you feel?

In the Mike Newell comedy-drama, *Four Weddings and a Funeral*, Carrie (Andie MacDowell) admits that she has had sex with thirty-three men. Charles (Hugh Grant) is stunned.

The conversation follows:

CARRIE: Anyway, I reckon I've had my fair run of it.
CHARLES: What is a fair run these days? Well, come on. Tell me. I've seen the [wedding] dress, we have no secrets now.
CARRIE: Well, the first one, of course, not easily forgotten, was kind of nice. Two, hairy back. Three, four...six was only a birthday, in my parent's room.
CHARLES: Which birthday?
CARRIE: Seventeen.
CHARLES: Oh, but, when you were just seventeen?
CARRIE: Well, you know, I grew up in the country, lots of rolling around in haystacks. Okay, seven, hum...
Eight, unfortunately was quite a shock..
CHARLES: Heh.
CARRIE: Nine, against a fence, very uncomfortable, don't try it.
CHARLES: I won't.
CARRIE: Ten, oh, gorgeous. Just heaven. Just, uh, he was wonderful.
CHARLES: I hate him.
CARRIE: Eleven...disappointing. Twelve through seventeen, university years, sensitive, caring, intelligent boys, sexually speaking, a real low patch.
CHARLES: Heh. Heh.
CARRIE: Eighteen, broke my heart, years of yearning.
CHARLES: I'm sorry.
CARRIE: Twenty, oh my God, I can't believe I've reached twenty. Twenty-one, elephant type. Twenty-two, kept falling asleep, that was my first year in England.
CHARLES: I do apologize.
CARRIE: Twenty-three and twenty-four together. That was something.
CHARLES: Seriously?

CARRIE: Twenty-seven, oh, that was a mistake.
CHARLES: Suddenly at twenty-seven, you make a mistake?
CARRIE: Yes, he kept screaming. It was very awful, and I nearly gave up on the whole thing, but Spencer changed my mind. That's twenty-eight. His father, twenty-nine.
CHARLES: His father?
CARRIE: Uh. Thirty, uh. Thirty-one, my God. Thirty-two was lovely. And then, my fiancé. That's thirty-three.
CHARLES: Wow! So, so, I came after your fiancé?
CARRIE: No, you were thirty-two.
CHARLES: Oh.
CARRIE: So there you go, less than Madonna, more than Princess Di, I hope. And how about you, how many have you slept with?
CHARLES: Christ!

Gramercy Pictures © 1994

How many former lovers is too many?

How would you feel if Your Beloved admitted to ten or twenty or thirty former lovers?

Do you worry that Your Beloved will compare you with former lovers?

Do you worry that Your Beloved will be unfaithful to you if he or she has had an active sex life before meeting you?

Do you worry about safe sex?

With sexually transmitted diseases and AIDS for which there are no cures, are you confident that Your Beloved takes and has taken every precaution?

Will you request that Your Beloved take an AIDS test prior to becoming intimate?

Have you or Your Beloved ever been treated for a sexually transmitted disease?

Have you or Your Beloved ever been tested for AIDS?
What were the results? When was the test conducted?
Do you doubt Your Beloved's faithfulness?
Have you asked Your Beloved to be tested recently?

After dating for several months, my boy friend told me that he had contracted herpes from a previous relationship. He said that he couldn't continue our relationship without telling me everything about himself, even if that "everything" was undesirable. He worried that I would break up with him. I valued his honesty. We were engaged two months later.

—Maxine

Have you or Your Beloved recently ended an affair?

How long ago did the affair end?

Do you or Your Beloved work with the ex?

Do you or Your Beloved see the ex socially?

Are you or Your Beloved tempted to call or see the ex?

Are you or Your Beloved still intimate with the ex?

Is this a stop gap relationship until things are patched up with the ex?

The way I remember the story, she had broken up with her boyfriend of many years. She began dating and immediately became pregnant with her new boyfriend. But she was still in love with her old boyfriend, so she begged him to take her back. He was delighted to have her back, baby and all. Furious and despondent, the jilted lover killed her old boyfriend and then himself. What a tragedy!

—Bob

What were the reasons you broke up with your ex?

Are any of these reasons likely to reappear in your relationship with Your Beloved?

Has Your Beloved ever been pregnant or involved with a pregnancy?

If so, was the child aborted? Or given up for adoption?

Are you willing to accept this child as your own?

Much to my surprise, my wedding present was a two-year-old son who had been mistreated by my husband's former live-in lover.

—Robin

Are you looking forward to being a full-time parent to a ready-made family?

Have you discussed how you feel with Your Beloved?

Has Your Beloved ever had an abortion? More than one?

How do you feel about this?

Will the abortion(s) make it difficult for Your Beloved to get pregnant?

> I never discussed my abortion with Bill. It really wasn't any of his business. After all it was my body.
>
> —Mariah

> I had two abortions by the time I met and married him. I told him about both of them.
>
> —Lucy

> I was young and scared and pregnant. I had the abortion because I didn't know what else to do. Afterwards, I felt so bad. I mean, I killed my baby!
>
> —Ronnie

Numerous prior sexual relationships significantly raise your exposure to sexual diseases, increase the risk of pregnancy outside of marriage (at last count, one-third of all children were born outside of marriage), and increase the probability of infidelity within this relationship.

Infidelity destroys marriages!

Commit now to a monogamous sexual relationship with Your Beloved. If Your Beloved is unable or unwilling to commit, this is definitely not your best choice!

MARRIAGE WORKS!

Chapter 26

Prior Marriages
Blended Families

Have either you or Your Beloved been married before? More than once before?

How many years was Your Beloved married?
How long has it been since the divorce?

I was married when I was eighteen. That marriage was annulled. It was such a bad experience that it's taken me years before I was willing to marry again.

—Meredith

This is my third marriage. He has never been married. My in-laws are more interested in my past than he is!

—Elaine

I got married at eighteen. I grew up on the wrong side of the tracks and was grateful to leave home. He had four kids for me to raise from his first marriage and then we had several of our own.

—Joan

> The first time I was too young and ignorant to know what I wanted. The second time I asked all the right questions and got all the right answers, but he lied to me. This is my third time and this time, it feels right!
>
> —Audrey

> I have been married six times. Somehow the courtship is always more exciting than the marriage.
>
> —Michael

Have you or Your Beloved completely recovered from your ex and are you emotionally ready for a new relationship?

Why did you or Your Beloved's previous marriage end in divorce? Explain in detail.

Did you or Your Beloved receive counseling after your divorce? If not, why?

Are these same issues or problems present in this relationship?

> We had to get married. We were both too young and too immature to deal with a marriage and a baby and work and school.
>
> —Barbie

> He was an addict. He would take all the money out of the bank and disappear for days at a time. Every time he'd come back, he'd swear he'd never do it again.
>
> —Karen

> He constantly criticized me. Nothing I did was ever good enough. When I was leaving him, he even criticized the way I packed my moving boxes. After twenty years, I had no self-esteem left.
>
> —Tessa

> He was abusive, both mentally and physically.
>
> —Rita

> He was so boring. He'd come home from work and sit in front of the TV and fall asleep. We never went anywhere or did anything. On week-ends, he worked on his car.
>
> —Nancy

> We had nothing in common. He liked to hunt and fish. He liked to hang out at bars. He liked to ride around on his motorcycle. He went to truck rallies and tractor pulls. He belonged to a bowling league. I hated all those things.
>
> —Ethel

> We had dated on and off for years. After awhile, everyone just expected that we would get married. I know she expected it. We didn't have anything in common. I had no business marrying her.
>
> —Mike

> She didn't want kids. I couldn't imagine married life without them.
>
> —Samuel

> That woman was a whore. When I found her in bed with a friend of mine, I kicked her out.
>
> —Will

> He tried to deny it. He had affairs the entire time we were married. He'd come in late or stay out all night or work weekends. I'd find bills for lingerie on our credit card, lipstick on his shorts. He said he loved me. He said he couldn't help it, his dad had affairs too.
>
> —Penny

What responsibilities do you still have to this former marriage?

Are you tied to your ex financially (alimony or child support)?

Did you have children from this former marriage?

Do you have child visitation rights? Or are you the primary caretaker of the children from your former marriage?

How will these responsibilities to your former marriage affect your new relationship with Your Beloved?

> After five marriages and several children, I keep track of birthdays and my visitation days on a lotus spread sheet.
>
> —Frank

> Paying alimony and child support keeps me financially strapped. My kids and ex always come first.
>
> —Earl

> I knew his children first and learned a lot about him before I ever met him. I knew children that great had to have a great dad!
>
> —Marie

> There are her kids. There are my kids. It is a ready-made family of ten.
>
> —Scott

> My son and his boys hated each other. It was a recipe for disaster!
>
> —Barbara

What is your relationship with your ex now? Was this a friendly divorce?

> We are still good friends; actually better friends now than when we were married.
>
> —Paul

> We all get together for holidays: my ex and his new wife, my former in-laws, whom I adore, my son and my live-in boy friend.
>
> —Shelly

> I couldn't stand it when we were married. Why would it be better now? Why would he be responsible and grown up now? Why would he stop drinking now? Why would we stop fighting? He's late to pick up the boys. Then he brings them back late; he forgets their birthdays. He schedules stuff and then doesn't show up. He's always nasty to me. I just get the boys settled down and then it's time for visitation again. Divorce didn't end anything. It just aggravated everything!
>
> —Patricia

> If I had shot him twenty years ago instead of marrying him, I would be better off financially and I would be out on parole by now.
>
> —Wilma

With up to fifty percent of all marriages ending in divorce (and an even higher divorce rate for remarriages), expectations of the couple who are getting married and expectations of their family and friends for a lifetime marriage are at an all time low!

In spite of the low expectations and negative attitudes swirling around you, do not lose sight of your goal: commitment to a lifetime marriage!

If you or Your Beloved have been married before, discuss the additional problems this raises: ex-husband or ex-wife, children, money, former in-laws.

Insist that Your Beloved commit now to a lifetime marriage with you. If Your Beloved is unable or unwilling to commit, this is not your best choice!

MARRIAGE WORKS!

Chapter 27

Religion

Are you religious? Is Your Beloved as religious as you are?

> We met in the church choir. Going to church and singing in the choir is very important to both of us.
>
> —Gary

> During our early married years, we were atheists. When our first child died, I turned to God for comfort. He buried himself in his work.
>
> —Opal

> For years, I went to church without him. I studied the Bible daily and I prayed that God would restore his faith. He told me that I was wasting my time. My prayers were answered. Now he goes to church with me.
>
> —Jenny

> He is a Unitarian, seeing only the human side of the Bible, the frailties and failures of the men and women in the Scriptures. I am a Fundamentalist, seeing only the divine. Any religious discussion leads to an argument.
>
> —Carol

Do you/Your Beloved believe in God?

Do you/Your Beloved belong to a church or synagogue?

Do you/Your Beloved attend church regularly (most Sundays/Saturdays)?

Or are you/Your Beloved C & E (Christmas and Easter) Christians?

Do you/Your Beloved read the Bible or other religious works daily?

Have you/Your Beloved committed many religious verses to memory?

Do you/Your Beloved have a daily prayer time?

Do you sing in the choir, volunteer for Vacation Bible School, serve on one of the church boards, teach Sunday School?

Were you/Your Beloved raised in the same religion?

Were you/Your Beloved baptized or confirmed as a child?

Did you/Your Beloved have a bar/bat mitzvah?

Are either of your parents ministers, rabbis, or religious leaders?

Have you attended church with Your Beloved?

Do you and Your Beloved plan to attend this same church after you are married?

Do you have religious discussions with Your Beloved?

If you are not of the same religion, how will you resolve this?

> One Sunday I go to his Catholic church; the next Sunday he goes to my Unitarian church.
>
> —Barb

> After being married for years, I converted from my Christian faith to Judaism to please my husband and his parents. We were remarried in a Jewish ceremony. I attend synagogue regularly and our children attend a private Jewish school. But I still hum Christmas carols in December.
>
> —Gina

> He was Jewish and I was Christian. After several dates, I visited him at his home. His folks were very pleasant. While I was there, his grandmother came over. His mother apologized but asked me to sit on the back porch until

> she left. "If she knew that Sidney were dating a Christian girl, she would be very upset." I didn't wait on the porch; I went home!
>
> —Amy

> My mom yelled: "You can't marry a Catholic! They don't believe in birth control so you'll have ten babies, the priests will tell you what to do, and you will have to eat fish on Friday. And you hate fish."
>
> —Carolyn

Will you join a nondenominational church?

Will you each go to your own church?

Will you convert to Your Beloved's religion or will he or she convert to yours?

And if the holidays are different, will you celebrate both sets of holidays or will you not celebrate at all?

If you have children, in what faith will the children be raised?

> We agreed to get married in the Catholic Church and we agreed to raise the children Catholic. I kept my end of the bargain. It was more important to her than to me.
>
> —Joe

> We agreed not to influence the children, so they weren't raised in any faith. We decided that they could choose for themselves when they grew up.
>
> —Bob

Were you or Your Beloved raised in a faith but are not practicing now?

Do you think you may return to your faith in the future?

> For years we slept in on Sundays. It was our only day to relax. But when I turned forty, I decided to go back to church. I went alone.
>
> —Camille

> I really wish my husband would go to church with me and the kids. 'Course his dad didn't go to church with his family either. I guess I should have known.
>
> —Roberta

> I was really really religious as a kid. I carried my rosary in a little pouch on my belt and when I didn't have anything else to do, I would pray. Over the years I lost that intensity, so it surprised me when I watched my husband search for his faith. He was so involved with the church that I felt left out.
>
> —Sandra

Religious compatibility cements a relationship. Unlike many other aspects of society, religion supports and encourages lifetime marriages.

Knowing that Your Beloved believes in basic religious tenets, attends religious services with you, and will encourage religious training for your children is very important.

If you were raised in two different religions, you must resolve any religious conflicts now. If these conflicts cannot be resolved, this is not your best choice.

If neither of you is involved in a religion now, it is possible that one or both of you may turn back to your faith when you get older, when your children are born, or in times of crisis.

Discuss the probability of your future interest in religion with Your Beloved.

Chapter 28

In Sickness and In Health

How healthy is Your Beloved?

Has Your Beloved been ill during the time you have been dating?

If so, with what?

I won't marry him because he isn't very healthy. I refuse to be his nurse when he is older and sicker.

—Emily

Does Your Beloved often have colds, backaches, headaches, stomach aches, constipation, allergies, sinus problems?

Is Your Beloved grumpy, whiny, silent, or mean while sick?

He never complains when he doesn't feel well.

—Lucy

She's always tired or has a headache or a backache or a stiff neck or an upset stomach or...She's always popping pills.

—Ron

What a baby! He whines and makes demands constantly: a pillow, a glass of water, a bowl of soup, a massage, music, company. And he always gives his illnesses to me!

—Janine

> He is always nursing some sports-related injury: the knee, the back, the ankle, the shoulder. He is always limping around and too injured to do any work around the house.
>
> —Olga

> Her dad was a hypochondriac, constantly suffering from imagined illnesses. She seemed healthy but I checked her medicine cabinet to see if it were stocked full of medicines. It wasn't.
>
> —Pete

Does Your Beloved have chronic illnesses or a serious disease: heart disease, diabetes, high blood pressure, sexually transmitted diseases, mental illness, cancer, or something else?

Has Your Beloved discussed this medical condition with you and are you aware of the seriousness of this problem?

Have you discussed this condition with his or her doctor?

Does Your Beloved take medication daily? What is the medication for?

Does Your Beloved take responsibility for this condition and follow the doctor's recommendations?

> It isn't my heart condition. It's his! I'm tired of being the police, watching his diet, his blood pressure levels, his exercise program, his alcohol consumption. Why can't he take care of himself?
>
> —Fran

> It's like pulling teeth to get him into the doctor's office for a regular checkup.
>
> —Nora

> He is really on top of this. He schedules all his own appointments and color codes all the pills he has to take.
>
> —Denise

> He has a bad heart, ulcers, high blood pressure, and depression. I cook low salt, low fat, bland foods for him. I always put out all his pills. Some days I feel like I am a nurse, not a wife.
>
> —Anita

Is Your Beloved genetically disposed to any diseases: asthma, heart disease, cancer, diabetes, mental illness (Alzheimers), glaucoma or macular degeneration, which may lead to blindness, or any other genetic diseases?

> The stroke robbed him of vision in one eye and untreated glaucoma stole the sight in his "good" eye. Now that he is legally blind, his wife put him into a nursing home. He was too much trouble. "What about me?" she said. I'm too old to be bothered with him."
>
> —Edna

> At 50, his mother began to suffer from asthma and all the medical conditions caused by the medications. Now my husband has asthma too.
>
> —Jane

> My mother had Alzheimers for years and died wheelchair bound, not recognizing me, not talking, and not feeding herself. Whenever I forgot something, my ex-husband would ask if I were "losing it too?"
>
> —Delores

Has Your Beloved had any serious operations? For what?

Was the condition corrected? Will any additional operations be necessary?

> She screamed at me when I had my triple bypass surgery. She was furious that I was so sick. I was causing her so much trouble. My doctor told me to divorce her because she was going to kill me with all her screaming.
>
> —Al

> Together we have so many ailments we keep the doctors busy. They keep patching us up and sending us home. We've got more pills than a pharmacy. We just take one day at a time now and spend it looking after each other.
>
> —John

Has Your Beloved been in any serious accidents? How did the accidents happen?

Were the accidents Your Beloved's fault?

Have the injuries healed completely?

> After falling twice in mountain climbing accidents, he agreed to give up the sport.
>
> —Ann

> I was in a serious car accident. It was months of rehab before I could take care of the kids or go back to work. He had to do everything.
>
> —Edna

> His grandfather worked the mines, so did his dad and his uncles and brothers. I pleaded with him to find another job but he refused.
>
> —Helen

Does Your Beloved have insomnia?

How many nights a week is this a problem?

Does Your Beloved take pills or alcohol to help him or her sleep?

> He never sleeps. We've tried everything: a new mattress, a cool room, tea, hot milk, exercise, no caffeine, acupuncture, counseling and drugs. Nothing works.
>
> —Nan

> I have to go to bed when she does, whether I'm tired or not. She is a very light sleeper and if I wake her up, she never goes back to sleep.
>
> —Dan

Does Your Beloved snore?

> We have tried every anti-snoring device known to man. The pillow, the sleeping position, the nose pincer, the Band-Aid, the herbal remedies, nose surgery. Nothing worked. Finally, I gave up and sleep in a separate bedroom.
>
> —Abigail

Has Your Beloved had cosmetic surgery? Why was it done?
Has Your Beloved had his or her teeth straightened?
Does Your Beloved have a bridge or false teeth?
Does Your Beloved wear contact lenses or glasses?

Does Your Beloved wear a hair piece or dye his or her hair?

Does Your Beloved have fake fingernails?

> She has these long red fingernails. They look like claws. She can't pick up small things, or open jars. She is constantly painting them or rebasing them or something. I despise them.
>
> —Rodney

Has Your Beloved had breast implants?

> He liked big-breasted women, so I had mine enlarged to please him. Now we are separated and I'm stuck with these big boobs.
>
> —Nina

Has Your Beloved had his or her nose bobbed or other cosmetic surgery?

Is Your Beloved pleased with the results? Are you?

> Many of the girls in my high school class had their noses bobbed or their breasts enlarged. They wanted to catch a husband in college.
>
> —Maya

> We both decided to have facelifts. After seeing all the trouble I had, he refused to do it. Now I look great and he looks ancient.
>
> —Janine

Are any additional cosmetic surgeries planned?

Has Your Beloved ever had skin cancer?

If so, does Your Beloved have regular check-ups now?

Does Your Beloved always wear suntan lotion, hat, and sunglasses when out in the bright sun?

> It wasn't machismo to wear suntan lotion. So every year he burned bright red. He ignored the bottles of sunblock and the articles on skin cancer. This year he had to have several cancerous growths removed from his face.
>
> —Phylis

If Your Beloved became seriously ill, are you willing to take care of him or her?

> Within a year of our marriage, he was diagnosed with a brain tumor. I watched him fade from a healthy vibrant man to a helpless invalid. I made special foods, held him when the pain pills wore off, and wept when he no longer recognized me. I was a widow at 22.
>
> —Sidney

> I demanded that he divorce me. I refused to become a burden to him. MS robbed me of my dreams but I wouldn't let it rob him too. Now he and his new wife and daughter visit me in the nursing home.
>
> —Alice

> She had a serious stroke and was wheelchair bound. I was determined to care for her as cheerfully and lovingly as she would have cared for me. She never complains and is always grateful for everything I do.
>
> —Jim

When you exchange your wedding vows, you will promise to love, honor, and cherish...in sickness and in health. This is a blind promise since you do not know what the future may hold.

Most couples make this promise when they are both young and in good health.

However, as you age, your good health may decline.

Your commitment to this lifetime relationship must be strong enough to overcome chronic illness, catastrophic accident, or mental incapacity.

Chapter 29

Maintain a Healthy Lifestyle

Does Your Beloved have a healthy lifestyle...plenty of exercise, reasonable diet, regular physicals, no addictions to tobacco, alcohol, or drugs?

Do you and Your Beloved practice good hygiene habits, regular showers, clean hair and nails, brushed teeth?

Does Your Beloved have a low energy level?

> There were TV sets in the kitchen, bedroom, and living room. My wife watched TV six to eight hours a day. Her life was planned around her special programs.
>
> —Robert

> He sleeps all the time. After sleeping eight to ten hours every night, my husband still naps during the day.
>
> —Dana

> Anytime I suggest doing something, she is always too tired.
>
> —Billy

> No one can keep up with her. She's a whirlwind.
>
> —Sam

Does Your Beloved accept responsibility for good health?

> He was a diabetic. He knew that he had to exercise, eat regularly, avoid alcohol and sugary foods, and monitor his medication carefully. He refused to do this. When I found him in a diabetic coma, I thought he was dead. I wasn't sad, I was furious!
>
> —Eileen

Does Your Beloved have regular physicals?

> My husband hates yearly physicals. It reminds him of his mortality.
>
> —Jill

Does Your Beloved exercise on a daily/weekly basis?

> He runs 35 to 40 miles a week. I think he's obsessed.
>
> —Karen

> She never exercises; she just overeats, and no surprise, she is overweight.
>
> —Hal

> It depends on the weather: golfing when it isn't snowing and skiing when it is.
>
> —Ruth

> He bought a treadmill, a stationary bike, a Healthrider, in-line skates and an abdomen "crunch" exerciser. Now all he has to do is use them.
>
> —Ginny

What sports activities is Your Beloved interested in?

> Except for racecar driving and mud wrestling, there isn't a sport that he doesn't play. His closet is filled with hockey sticks, golf clubs, scuba gear, basketballs, bowling balls, baseballs, skis, skates, and gravity boots.
>
> —Hanna

Do you exercise together? How strenuous is your exercise?

Before we were married, we jogged together. Now she never wants to exercise with me. It's really lonely running without her.

—Jeff

We met on a bowling league and really enjoy our bowling nights.

—Ellie

Are you willing to learn a sport Your Beloved enjoys?

I love handball. She refused to play hand ball. "Who would want to play this game? Every time I hit the ball my hand hurts."

—Dave

She wept going up the ski lift because she was so scared. I thought she would wait until spring before coming back down.

—Bill

Is Your Beloved overweight? Five, ten, twenty, fifty pounds overweight?

He is at least eighty pounds overweight and is on high blood pressure and high cholesterol medication. I prepare diet foods and he sneaks cookies, ice cream and whoppers. When he refuses to stay on his diet, I get furious!

—Addie

Is Your Beloved on an exercise and diet program now?

Is Your Beloved always dieting?

Has Your Beloved been overweight most of his or her life?

Does Your Beloved take diet pills or just not eat?

Is Your Beloved willing to alter eating habits to keep at approved weight chart levels?

Are you willing to help Your Beloved reach this goal by cooking diet foods and changing your own eating habits?

I didn't know that she had lost fifty pounds before I met her. Within a year of marriage, she had gained them all back.

—Hank

> She never dieted. She just watched her weight, ate sensibly, and exercised. After thirty years of marriage, she still looks great.
>
> —Jake

> I have tried every diet program and diet pill there is...without success. I weigh more now than ever.
>
> —Darla

> I was diagnosed with dangerously high blood pressure. The doctor insisted that I lose at least forty pounds. The new diet was low fat and low salt. My wife refused to cook special meals for me ("that's too much work") and she refused to feed the entire family the low fat/low salt recipes ("if you want it, you can fix it yourself"). My medication has increased and I have gained more weight.
>
> —Tom

Does Your Beloved have an eating disorder (anorexia, bulimia)? Has Your Beloved ever had an eating disorder in the past? Is he or she willing to accept counseling to resolve this problem?

> At twelve she was anorexic. Now after counseling and medication, she is completely recovered.
>
> —Jim

In Andrew Morton's book, *Diana – Her True Story – In Her Own Words*, Princess Di admitted to being bulimic on her honeymoon.

"By then the bulimia was appalling, absolutely appalling. It was rife, four times a day on the yacht. Anything I could find I would gobble up and be sick two minutes later.

"So, of course, that slightly got the mood swings going in the sense that one minute one would be happy, next blubbing one's eyes out."

Does Your Beloved have any food or drug allergies? List them.

> After a trip to the emergency room, I made him wear a dog tag stating that he was allergic to penicillin.
>
> —Beth

> I never knew that he was allergic to shellfish. I made him shrimp creole for his birthday and he couldn't eat it
>
> —Amanda

> I didn't know that he was allergic to peanuts and sent him some homemade candy. I could have killed him.
>
> —Bev

Do you/Your Beloved take vitamins? Which ones?

> He probably takes fifty to sixty vitamins a day. I can't believe that all those pills are necessary.
>
> —Joy

Is Your Beloved a hypochondriac, turning every headache into a brain tumor?

> Never say to Dwayne, "How are you?" He will give you a ten-minute discussion on every medical problem he is currently facing...hangnail, fever blister, stiff neck, gas, toothache...it's so boring.
>
> —Gail

Medical researchers agree that a healthy lifestyle will discourage diseases and illnesses.

If you and Your Beloved are physically active, sports-oriented, not overweight, and not addicted to tobacco, alcohol, or drugs, and committed to a healthy lifestyle, your chances of enjoying good health into your elderly years greatly increases.

MARRIAGE WORKS!

Chapter 30

Addictions

Does Your Beloved currently smoke cigarettes, cigars, a pipe or chew tobacco? Do you?

> Henry smokes constantly. He coughs and coughs, then lights up another cigarette. Everything in the house smells like smoke, even my clothes. And I never smoke.
>
> —Lorraine

For how many years has Your Beloved used a tobacco product? Has Your Beloved ever tried to quit?

> First he smoked cigarettes. Then he smoked a pipe. That pipe was always in his mouth. A routine physical uncovered throat cancer. He died a year later.
>
> —Rose

Does Your Beloved have any current plans to quit?
Have you asked Your Beloved to quit?
What was the response?

> I smoked when we got married but he didn't, so I quit.
>
> —Lynn

> He has tried to stop chewing tobacco so many times. But he started when he was fourteen and I guess he will die chewing.
>
> —Zoe

If you do not smoke, do you mind if Your Beloved does? Will you establish "house rules" for smoking?

Do Your Beloved's parents smoke? Do yours?

Will you have house rules restricting visiting relatives from smoking in your home?

> My in-laws were furious when I asked them to smoke out on the deck.
>
> —Bob

Does Your Beloved drink alcohol? Do you?

> He was drunk when we met. And he stayed drunk for our entire marriage. My dad was an alcoholic. I can't believe I ignored all the signs.
>
> —Phoebe

> We didn't have any fun unless we were drunk. We spent years in an alcoholic stupor. I drank through my pregnancies. I drank to be happy. I drank when I was sad or mad. After a while, I didn't need a reason to drink.
>
> —Nancy

How much alcohol does Your Beloved drink?

How often: Daily? Weekly? Wine with dinner for a special occasion? Nightly beers or hard liquor to unwind? Drinks with the guys? Drinks at lunch?

Does Your Beloved have to have an alcoholic drink to feel comfortable and have a good time?

During the time you have been dating, has Your Beloved ever been drunk or hung over? How many times?

Is Your Beloved ever abusive or violent when drinking?

Does Your Beloved pressure you to drink alcohol too?

> Alcohol makes me sick. He insisted that I drink with him. When I refused to drink, he got really mad.
>
> —Darla

Is Your Beloved addicted to alcohol?

> I really love him but I can't live with an alcoholic anymore. His drinking is destroying our family.
>
> —Jean

Has Your Beloved ever been in an alcoholic rehab center? More than once?

Ask Your Beloved to discuss the circumstances of being in a rehab center with you.

> He has been in and out of rehab centers more times than I can remember. He will keep it together for a while and then he will take all the money out of the bank and go off on a bender.
>
> —Sadie

Has Your Beloved ever asked you to lie for him or her to cover up a drinking problem?

Has Your Beloved ever appeared drunk at work?

Has Your Beloved ever lost a job because of drinking?

Has Your Beloved ever had a DUI conviction? More than once?

Ask Your Beloved to discuss the circumstances of losing the job or getting the DUI with you.

Are you concerned with the amount of alcohol Your Beloved drinks now?

Have you asked Your Beloved to cut back or to stop drinking alcohol?

Are you willing to marry Your Beloved knowing that he or she abuses alcohol?

Has Your Beloved resolved a drinking problem and joined AA? How long has Your Beloved been sober?

Do you believe that Your Beloved will be able to remain sober?

> My parents never had alcohol in our house. Neither my husband nor I drink and we don't serve it at parties. Our friends wonder if we are recovering alcoholics or Mormons.
>
> —Josy

Does Your Beloved abuse prescription drugs?

> It started with back pain. Now she pops those painkillers constantly.
>
> —Norman

> He couldn't sleep. He tripled the prescription dosage and he still doesn't sleep.
>
> —Nancy

Has Your Beloved ever used illegal drugs? Have you?
Which ones? How often?
Are you or Your Beloved using illegal drugs now?
Are you or Your Beloved addicted?

> When he came home from Viet Nam, he was a changed man. He was hooked on heroin. I took the baby and left.
>
> —Lois

Has Your Beloved been in a drug rehab facility?

How many times has Your Beloved completed the rehab program?

Discuss the details of Your Beloved's stay in the rehab center.

How long has Your Beloved been off drugs?

Is Your Beloved ever abusive when using drugs?

If you don't use drugs, does Your Beloved pressure you to use drugs too?

Has Your Beloved ever appeared at work high on drugs?

Has Your Beloved failed drug tests or been fired for drug use?

Has Your Beloved ever asked you to lie to cover up drug use?

> He used drugs for years. And I covered up for him. I'd call work and say he was sick. I'd tell the children he was working late. I'd tell his mom he'd call her later. Drugs were the most important things in his life.
>
> —Gail

Has Your Beloved been arrested for possessing illegal drugs?
Has Your Beloved ever sold drugs?

Has Your Beloved been convicted for selling drugs?

Are you willing to have Your Beloved continue using drugs after you're married?

If Your Beloved is using drugs now, will she/he agree to stop using illegal drugs and enter a rehab center?

Do you believe Your Beloved will be able to end his or her habit?

Discuss this issue with Your Beloved.

> I was an alcoholic and he was a drug user. We both agreed to give up our habits when we got married. Neither of us could keep this promise. I started using drugs with him.
>
> —Jenna

Addictions may take many different forms. Your Beloved may be addicted to alcohol, drugs, gambling, tobacco, sex.

Regardless of the type of addiction, the self-absorbed, single-minded pursuit of the addiction will destroy your relationship. The addiction will also destroy Your Beloved's life goals, his or her relationship with family and friends, financial status, and ability to work. There is no room for addictions in a committed relationship.

Look for the signs of addiction; if you suspect Your Beloved is addicted, confront him or her.

If Your Beloved agrees on treatment, postpone your marriage plans until you are convinced that Your Beloved is free from addictions.

If Your Beloved is unsuccessful in giving up this addiction or unwilling to seek treatment, this is not your best choice!

MARRIAGE WORKS!

Chapter 31

What You See Is What You Get!

How do you plan to change Your Beloved?

> She wanted to donate my favorite records of railroad train sounds to a charity.
>
> —Jordan

> She wanted me to give up my struggling career as a musician to join her father's construction company.
>
> —Harry

> He wanted me to dress more conservatively. Those revealing clothes were all right before we got married but not now!
>
> —Jessie

> I want him to drink less and give up smoking. He wants me to give up illegal drugs.
>
> —Alice

> He wants me to lose weight, exercise and eat healthy foods.
>
> —Stella

> He wants me to give up my career, stay home, and make babies. So why exactly did I get my MBA?
>
> —Jill

If these reconstruction efforts don't work, will that damage or destroy your marriage?

Were these changes discussed before the wedding?

> I never saw it coming. I had no idea she planned to remake me. She expects me to give up my friends ("too boring"), my red meat ("too fattening"), my beer ("too addicting") and my baseball team ("too time-consuming").
>
> —Ted

Of course you love Your Beloved. But you may not like some of his or her habits. Even your best choice isn't perfect. Be honest. List five annoying habits Your Beloved has.

1.
2.
3.
4.
5.

Have you discussed these habits with Your Beloved?

What did Your Beloved say?

Was Your Beloved willing to change?

Was Your Beloved annoyed with your comments?

Did Your Beloved have a list of your annoying habits to discuss too?

If these habits remain unchanged, will they detract from your relationship with Your Beloved?

If these habits remain unchanged, will they cause arguments?

> After every meal, he clicks and sucks on his teeth. Click. Click. Click. Click. It drives me to distraction.
>
> —Ellie

> He drinks from the milk carton, leaves dirty dishes around the house, burps loudly, leaves stacks of newspapers and

> magazines in the bathroom, never puts the lid of the toilet down, snores, and is never on time. But he is loving, committed to our relationship, a good provider, funny, smart, and hard working! I love him, warts and all.
>
> —Lois

> She spends hours getting ready-hair, makeup, clothes, nails. She is always late.
>
> —Rodney

> She constantly interrupts me, carries on conversations with others when I'm talking, and finishes my sentences for me.
>
> —Bob

Assume that these annoying habits will never change. Do you wish to continue with this relationship?

> She wanted me to change. I told her "WYSIWYG!" (What you see is what you get!).
>
> —Stan

I Love You, You're Perfect, Now Change is the title of a musical revue by Joe DiPietro that sums up the situation you may be facing. Many couples have a few changes in mind that haven't been discussed: throwing out the ratty sweater or chair, changing the tacky haircut or flashy car, giving away the yappy little dog, diluting the personality quirks, turning off the train music, and demanding that the annoying bad habits end.

Assume that Your Beloved will not change! Also assume that you will spend a lifetime with Your Beloved, including these irritating habits. If these irritations erase all the good qualities that you see in Your Beloved, then this is not your best choice.

MARRIAGE WORKS!

Chapter 32

Stressed? Who's Stressed?

Do you look forward to seeing Your Beloved at the end of each day?

Are you able to discuss the "happenings" of the day?
Is Your Beloved interested in your stories?
Can Your Beloved relate to your day?

> We were married for twenty-two years. I quit telling him about my work years ago. He really wasn't interested and couldn't relate to my computer business.
>
> —Colleen

> We are both doctors. He works in a small family practice and I work in a hospital emergency room. It really helps to discuss medical issues.
>
> —Leila

> I'm the housewife. He's the office manager. He doesn't want to hear about the clogged drain, the color of Ryan's poop, or changing the wallpaper.
>
> —Susie

Does Your Beloved know the names of your co-workers, club members, classmates?

Do you include Your Beloved in your work day whenever possible? Lunches? Office parties?

Is Your Beloved a workaholic or a perfectionist?

Does he or she expect you to live up to his or her strenuous standards?

Does he or she constantly correct you, advise you, instruct you, cross-examine you, criticize you?

Does Your Beloved suggest that you should do it over again his or her way?

> I love to talk to him. He is always so sensible and so loving. He always comes up with great solutions to every problem.
>
> —Lisa

> He criticized me constantly. Nothing I ever did was good enough. The house was never clean enough; the food was too spicy or too cold or nothing he liked. The shirts were never ironed right. I cried too much. I was too silly or too lazy or too fat or too ____. You fill in the blank.
>
> —Ronda

> He gave me a list of chores each morning. If I sat down for a minute or answered the phone to talk to a friend, he would say, "Don't you have some chores to do?"
>
> —Louise

> She monitored my entire life. She picked my clothes, my friends, my career. I moved through life on autopilot.
>
> —Larry

Does Your Beloved have a lot of stress in his or her life?

> He works in his family's business. He works long hours for very little money. He can never please them. When he gets angry with them, he takes it out on me.
>
> —Dawn

> Money is always tight. We are always over our budget and always owe money on our credit cards. We always fight over finances.
>
> —Alvin

> His ex-wife and children demand a lot of time and money. She has attempted suicide several times just to get his attention.
>
> —Joan

> Stress? You name it. We've got it. His ex. My ex. His sick mother. My overbearing mother. His boss. My boss. His travel schedule. My children. Our finances. The puppy. The broken furnace. More finances. The stealing of my car. My alcoholic sister. His brother and family moving in with us.
>
> —Marty

List the issues that currently cause stress.

1.
2.
3.

Are any of the issues related to you?

How will these issues affect your relationship?
Will any of these issues continue after you are married?
Will other stressful issues arise after you are married?

List the issues that will cause stress after you are married.

1.
2.
3.

Stress is unavoidable. It will appear in many different forms during your lifetime together: illnesses, in-law irritations, children's misbehavior, financial problems, job changes, moves, holidays, and so on.

However, if Your Beloved increases your level of stress rather than defuses it, this is not your best choice!

MARRIAGE WORKS!

Chapter 33

Communication

Does Your Beloved have a sense of humor?

> I didn't marry him because he was handsome or rich. I married him because he could make me laugh!
>
> —Martha

Does Your Beloved whine?

> What a turnoff! A 250-pound whiner.
>
> —Ann

Does Your Beloved interrupt you and finish your sentence?

Is Your Beloved impatient for you to finish so he or she can do all the talking?

Does Your Beloved talk too much? Not enough?

> She never stops talking...clothes, the kids, her parents, her friends, the house. Can't she ever talk about something interesting?
>
> —Stewart

> If I hear more than seven words during the evening I'm lucky. "Yup, nope, I dunno, maybe, okay, uh huh." He says I talk enough for both of us.
>
> —Bea

Does Your Beloved's conversation consist of lines from movies?

Do you mind?

> "Love means never having to say you're sorry." "Life is like a box of chocolates." "You make me want to be a better man." You get the idea.
>
> —Rachel

Does Your Beloved "converse" with you by asking rapid-fire questions?

> His method of communicating is by asking questions. We don't have a conversation. We have cross-examination and I'm the hostile witness.
>
> —Norma

Is Your Beloved's conversation boring?

> What's for dinner? My supervisor is a bitch. Is it big enough for you? He asks the same questions all the time.
>
> —Millie

Is Your Beloved condescending or argumentative?

Does Your Beloved criticize your actions and tell you what you should have done?

Is Your Beloved jealous?

> He checked my car speedometer to see where I had driven; he had access to my e-mail password and my answering machine and checked all my messages; he drove past my work to be sure I was there; he monitored my girlfriends and once he beat up an ex boyfriend.
>
> —Eva

You will spend a lifetime talking with Your Beloved. Practice good communication skills now! Don't interrupt. Don't ignore issues that are sensitive to discuss. Share your hopes and dreams with Your Beloved. Share your fears, stress, and feelings of frustration. No one should be more interested in communicating with you than Your Beloved.

If this isn't the case, this is not your best choice.

In a committed relationship of equals, there is no room for mental abuse. Do not tolerate condescension, jealousy, or attacks on your self-esteem.

Confront Your Beloved. If he or she is unwilling to treat you and your ideas with respect, this is not your best choice.

MARRIAGE WORKS!

Chapter 34

Manage Your Anger

Everyone has disastrous-not good-loathsome-awful-bad-bad-demon days when nothing planned works out. Have you ever been with Your Beloved when he or she is experiencing this type of day? Was Your Beloved mildly annoyed, upset, angry, worried, furious, ballistic, resigned, in control, or livid?

Did Your Beloved blame you for the problem?

Was it Your Beloved's fault?

Was it your fault? Someone else's fault or no one's fault?

If it were Your Beloved's fault, did he or she accept responsibility for the problem?

If it were your fault, did you accept responsibility for the problem and apologize?

How did you react to Your Beloved's handling of the situation?

Did the problem cause you to argue?

How was it resolved?

Is it likely to occur again?

Were you able to discuss the problem at the time?

Were you able to discuss the problem later?

Were you able to laugh about the problem?

> It had rained for days. The car broke down. I had a cold. The boss yelled at me and it wasn't my fault. I lost my wallet. The cleaning fell off the hanger into a puddle. I arrived at my boyfriend's apartment in a foul state. He was wonderful. He put his arms around me and held me. I instantly felt much better!
>
> —Kathy

> He was angry when he picked me up. Then when we were cut off in traffic; he lost it. He yelled obscenities, drove really fast and close to the other cars. He scared me to death.
>
> —Georgia

> He refuses to get upset. He says, "No worries."
>
> —Beth

> He has a hair-trigger temper. He's worse when he is drinking. The least little thing will set him off. It's impossible to guess when he will blow up next.
>
> —Jan

> We screamed at each other a lot when we were dating. And we scream at each other a lot now that we are married. But we never stay mad long.
>
> —Flo

> She is the calmest person I know. The world will come crashing down on her and she just deals with it.
>
> —Tim

Does Your Beloved lose his or her temper often?

How often? Hourly? Daily? Weekly? Yearly?

Have you been with Your Beloved on some occasions when he or she is angry?

Does Your Beloved become angry to intimidate you and to get his or her own way?

Can you tell when Your Beloved is angry?

Does he or she clench or grind teeth, glare, yell, curse, throw objects, slam down objects, sulk, walk away, or refuse to talk?

When angry, does Your Beloved become physically or

mentally abusive or violent?

> I wanted to go out for a lovely Valentine's dinner. He gave me roses and a box of candy. He refused to have dinner with me and instead went out with his friends. He came home drunk. I was angry because he had ruined my dinner plans. He got angry when I yelled at him and cut off the heads of all the roses and dumped the chocolates into the garbage.
>
> —LuAnn

> I never know when he might explode. I tiptoe around hoping to avoid confrontations.
>
> —Anita

> He argues with me until I agree with him. Any viewpoint except his is not tolerated.
>
> —Belinda

Do you and Your Beloved have frequent arguments or screaming matches?

What is the reason for your most frequent arguments?
Sex? Money? In-laws? Children? Politics?
His ex? Your ex?
What else?

> We argued a lot about money. I wanted to save it. He wanted to spend it. We finally agreed to discuss all expenditures over $50.00.
>
> —Becky

> Sex. Sex. Sex. Too much! Not enough! That about sums it up.
>
> —Todd

> Every Sunday he visits his mother and sisters. He always comes home angry and starts an argument with me.
>
> —Anita

> He'd take me to a party and then spend all his time talking and dancing with everyone but me. That made me real mad.
>
> —Yolanda

She is always late. Always!

—Eddie

She never wants to leave the kids with the baby sitter and go out. She says she doesn't spend enough time with them as it is. I think she hovers and smothers.

—Harold

My mother-in-law interrupts my life with constant criticism, complaints, and unsolicited advice. I call her "She Who Can't Be Pleased!"

—Miriam

My husband's mother Jeri can be unpleasant and occasionally mean-spirited. I was really angry when my husband told me I had "jerrybuilt" a project. I thought he was comparing me to his mother! I didn't accept his apology until he showed me the word in the dictionary!

—Lindsey

Briefly list your last five arguments.

1.
2.
3.
4.
5.

Were you both pleased by the way these arguments were resolved?
How often do these arguments occur?
Do they occur at the same time of day?

He comes home from work and sits in front of the TV. I am trying to make dinner, feed the kids and the dog, pick up a little, put groceries away, and he just sits and watches TV.

—Laverne

Every time his mother visits we have a huge argument.

—Bonnie

Is it possible to resolve any of these arguments?

Do you set a time later in the day when you have both cooled down and can discuss the problem without anger?

Everyone gets angry and loses his or her temper, even Your Beloved. If this is a frequent occurrence, if the anger is out of proportion to the problem, if it is a problem that you can't change, you must discuss it with Your Beloved when he or she is not angry.

Without an apology, without discussion, without a plan to avoid or accept this situation in the future, your relationship will suffer.

If this is a continuing problem, urge Your Beloved to attend anger-management classes. If Your Beloved is unable or unwilling to change, this is not your best choice.

MARRIAGE WORKS!

Chapter 35

For Better or For Worse

Do you enjoy arguing with each other?

> We fight all the time. It's the only way we know how to communicate.
>
> —Lou

Do you practice fair fighting rules?

(1) Discuss the problem when you aren't angry.
(2) Don't expect Your Beloved to "read your mind."
(3) Don't give Your Beloved the silent treatment.
(4) Limit the time spent on the argument.
(5) Always stick to the problem.
(6) Don't dredge up old arguments.
(7) No name calling or swearing.
(8) No nasty comments about each other or family.
(9) Be ready to say "I'm sorry" and "I forgive you."

Are there other rules you might add to personalize your fair fighting list?

Balanced against your future together, how important is this argument?

Some couples only communicate by arguing. Do not limit your conversations to taunting, teasing, belittling, picking on, or humiliating.

Remember this is a relationship of equals. Practice the fair fighting rules.

Always resolve the argument, even if you are forced to postpone the discussion until you are less angry. Winning the argument isn't the issue; resolving the problem is!

Always end by saying "I'm sorry" and "I forgive you."

Chapter 36

Abusive Actions

Do arguments ever escalate into pushing, shoving, hitting, kicking, spitting, biting, or throwing or breaking things? Have you ever been afraid for your own safety?

Has Your Beloved ever mentally, physically or sexually abused you?

> He physically abused me even before we got married. Two weeks before the wedding we got into a fight and I got a black eye. I wore heavy makeup on my wedding day and I wrote thank-you notes for wedding gifts he had broken in the fight!
>
> —Martha

> We had terrible screaming fights before we married but he never physically abused me. He saved that for after the wedding!
>
> —Shelley

> She threw anything she could get her hands on when she was angry.
>
> —Frank

> After an argument, he would be silent for days. Then it would all blow over and he would act like nothing had happened.
>
> —Lynn

> You know the Bible says not to let the sun set on your anger. That has always worked for me.
>
> —Will

Has Your Beloved ever lost a job, had an accident, been in a serious fight, been injured, injured someone else, or been jailed because he or she became angry? If yes, have Your Beloved explain this to you.

Has Your Beloved ever had anger-management counseling to resolve this problem?

If not, is Your Beloved willing to attend anger-management classes?

In a relationship of equals, every issue can be discussed without fear. If arguments with Your Beloved disintegrate into physical, sexual, or mental abuse, you must end the relationship immediately! This is not your best choice!

Chapter 37
Mental Health

Is Your Beloved depressed?

Is Your Beloved overly emotional, withdrawn or listless?

Has Your Beloved been in therapy in the past or is he or she currently in therapy?

Have you ever talked with his or her therapist or attended any of these counseling sessions?

Is Your Beloved on medication to control a mental problem?

What medication does Your Beloved take and what is it for?

What will happen if Your Beloved stops taking this medication?

Has Your Beloved or any member of the family been treated or institutionalized for mental illness?

> Keeping up with his mood swings was exhausting. He'd invite friends over when he was manic and by the time they arrived he was depressed. He'd have a temper tantrum and they'd all go home.
>
> —Ethel

His mom has been in and out of mental hospitals all his life with a bipolar disorder.

—Angie

He had a nervous breakdown before we were married. I thought it was caused by military service. Later he was diagnosed schizophrenic. Medication only helped a little. Finally he committed suicide.

—Ann

Every few weeks she'd cry, rage, and sulk. She said it was PMS. She said all women acted this way. I don't remember my mother or sisters acting this way.

—John

Is Your Beloved manic depressive or suicidal?

Has Your Beloved ever attempted suicide? When and why?

Have Your Beloved discuss this with you in detail!

If suicide was attempted, did Your Beloved receive counseling after this attempt?

Is Your Beloved likely to attempt suicide again?

Her mental health has been an issue for our entire marriage. She has taken anti-depressants for years. When they no longer worked, she was institutionalized. Electric shock treatments seem to help.

—Joe

My mom would climb up on the roof and threaten to kill herself. This was such a regular event that no one took it seriously. But I guess she was probably crazy.

—Marge

He found his dad dead with a shotgun blast to his head.

—Ali

If Your Beloved struggles with mental illness, you must obtain all the information possible about the illness, the medication, and the impact this issue will have on the future of your relationship. In some instances, mental illness is hereditary; how has this affected Your Beloved's family? Will this issue affect your decision to have children? If you are unable or unwilling to face these issues over a lifetime, end your relationship now.

Chapter 38

Crime and Consequences

Does Your Beloved have a criminal record?
What was the crime?
Was it a misdemeanor or a felony?
How much time did he or she serve in jail?
Was he or she released early on good behavior?
Did this occur as a juvenile or as an adult?
Has Your Beloved explained the reasons for the crime?

Has Your Beloved received counseling, anger management, alcohol, or drug rehab to avoid the recurrence of a criminal act?

Is Your Beloved still friends with the criminals he or she knew before he or she was imprisoned?

Is Your Beloved a repeat offender?

Are the circumstances that led to the crime likely to be repeated once you are married?

How will Your Beloved's prison record affect his or her ability to get a job and support your family?

Will it affect your relationship in other ways?

Has Your Beloved continued his or her life of crime?

Is Your Beloved a member of a gang?

Does he or she expect you to assist him or her in these criminal acts?

> I met him when he was in prison. We corresponded for years. I sent him hundreds of dollars to pay for his appeals (unsuccessful) and other expenses. Later I found out he corresponded with other women who sent him money too. My friends warned me about him. Why didn't I see that he was a loser?
>
> —Jillian

> He was a real charmer. We all liked him. My dad even liked him and he never liked anyone I dated. We didn't know about his past, including a prison record for assault.
>
> —Bea

> He had been in trouble as a teenager...stealing, drugs, DUI. After several months in jail, he decided to turn his life around. He gave up his old crowd, goes to AA, goes to church, has two jobs and plans for college. I know he will make it.
>
> —Sonia

> I knew he was a drug dealer. I told him, "Just don't tell me. I don't want to know nothing about it."
>
> —Sally

If Your Beloved has a criminal record, you must decide if this criminal behavior will destroy your relationship. If the crime is violent in nature, end the relationship now; this is not your best choice! If the criminal behavior is habitual, end the relationship now; this is not your best choice! If Your Beloved continues his or her friendships with other criminals, it is unlikely that he or she will end this criminal behavior; this is not your best choice!

If, however, this was a juvenile offense or a nonviolent misdemeanor that occurred years ago and has never been repeated, you must decide if Your Beloved has reformed. If Your Beloved has a steady job, new friends, no addictions, or an untreated mental illness and a genuine desire to leave this life of crime, postpone your wedding plans until you are certain that Your Beloved has reformed or recovered (*i.e.*, mental illness).

Chapter 39

Siblings and Friends

Have you spent time with all Your Beloved's brothers and sisters? Did you enjoy them and look forward to seeing them again?

His brother truly was one of the most disagreeable people I have ever met. He lived with us for months, never paid back the money he borrowed, never held down a job, and constantly belittled me.

—May

He has four brothers and two sisters. I have three sisters. We always have a crowd with them, all the husbands and children. Now our children are all good friends too.

—Evelyn

She dislikes her older sister and hasn't spoken to her for years.

—Greg

He warned me about his older sister. And he was right. She really is a witch. She somehow ruins all our get-togethers.

—Amy

He cut off his family years ago.

—Ann

Do you and Your Beloved share the same group of friends? If a different group of friends, have you met Your Beloved's friends?

Has Your Beloved had these friends for years (high school or college friends)? Or are they new friends?

Are they business friends?

Does Your Beloved have many friends or a few close friends?

Does Your Beloved have no friends and rely on you for all social interaction?

Does Your Beloved resent you having friends and try to break up these friendships? If so, have you discussed this with Your Beloved?

Does Your Beloved consider his or her brothers and sisters close friends?

Does Your Beloved look and sound like his or her friends or siblings: haircut, clothes, religion, politics, ambitions?

Does Your Beloved quote his or her friends often?

Does Your Beloved rely on these friends to make his or her decisions?

Does Your Beloved meet with his or her friends often?

Are there specific times set aside for shopping or lunches or bowling and baseball teams or poker games?

Are these dancing/drinking/bar-hopping friends?

Will these activities continue to be appropriate once you are married?

Are you included in any of these events?

Do you attend? Was it a success?

Are any of Your Beloved's friends ex-boyfriends or ex-girlfriends, ex-husbands or ex-wives?

Do you dislike Your Beloved seeing his or her ex?

Do you expect this to continue after you're married?

Have you discussed this with Your Beloved?

Are you comfortable with Your Beloved's friends and do you enjoy their company?

Have you spent any time alone with Your Beloved's friends?

Have Your Beloved's friends ever said or done anything that made you uncomfortable?

If so, did you discuss this with Your Beloved?

Did Your Beloved take your concerns seriously?

Did Your Beloved speak to his or her friends about your concerns?

> Several of his friends asked me to sleep with them. I was appalled. He thought it was funny!
>
> —Agnes

> One of her friends kept brushing against me and giving me that "Let's get it on" look. It made me really uncomfortable. When I told her about it, she decided that she would only see her for girlfriend nights.
>
> —Jeff

How does Your Beloved treat his or her friends?

If Your Beloved becomes disappointed or angry with a friend, how does he or she resolve the problem?

Does Your Beloved cut them off, discuss the problem, pretend the incident didn't happen, or bad mouth the friend?

> Whenever she got angry with friends, she would cut them off. I try very hard not to make her mad. I wonder if she'd dump me?
>
> —Steve

> He was very logical and low key. He would discuss the problem right away. Nothing was ever left to fester.
>
> —Jean

> Nothing her girlfriends did ever made her mad. Once a friend borrowed her favorite pink sweater for a date. When they were making out in the woods, a skunk sprayed them. Her sweater stunk so badly that it was buried. She thought it was funny!
>
> —Arnie

Do you want Your Beloved to spend less time with friends after your marriage?

How much less time?

Have you discussed this with Your Beloved?
What was his or her reaction?

> He thought it was perfectly all right to spend the weekend watching football games with his friends because I was invited too. I hate football.
>
> —Mary

> He has a standing poker game with several friends once a month. Nothing interferes with poker game nights.
>
> —Fran

Has Your Beloved met your friends?

Have you specifically asked your friends or siblings for their opinion of Your Beloved?

What did they say?

Do your friends or siblings like Your Beloved? If not, why not? Do you agree with their opinion? How important is it to you if your friends or siblings don't like Your Beloved?

> "You can do better, dear!" my mother said.
>
> —Clare

> My friends said, "Well, if you like her. But she wouldn't be my choice."
>
> —Stan

> His mom told him, "What a lovely young lady!"
>
> —Roberta

> "That young man is perfect for you," my girlfriend told me.
>
> —Ginger

> He was so handsome and articulate. She was plump, plain and provincial. None of us understood what he saw in her!
>
> —Sharon

> If my friends had REALLY told me what they thought of her, I never would have married her. NEVER!
>
> —Larry

> After I was divorced, all my friends told me that he was a loser, a two-timing cheat, a jerk, a drunkard. Why didn't they tell me this before I got married?
>
> —Molly

Will you be forced to choose between your friends or siblings and Your Beloved?

Have your friends met Your Beloved's friends?

Do your friends and Your Beloved's blend well?

Will you ever entertain the two groups of friends at the same time?

> I am a computer nerd. She is a rodeo princess. My friends are "hackers;" hers are "horsey." There wasn't anything in common!
>
> —Gene

Have you and Your Beloved made new friends together?

Once you are married, you will form a new circle—your parents, your brothers and sisters, your friends, Your Beloved and Your Beloved's parents, brothers and sisters, and friends.

Unless you move far away from all your friends and both your families, you will be spending holidays, vacations, and outings with these people.

If you are actively disliked, if you are uncomfortable with these people, if you can't imagine spending a lifetime with these people, this may not be your best choice!

MARRIAGE WORKS!

Chapter 40

Play Together

I got married so I'd never be lonely again! I would always have someone to play with. Now she says she's too busy to play.

—Hank

Describe your/Your Beloved's idea of a "perfect" evening together. Discuss this!

She loves crowds of friends, bright lights, excitement, and loud music. I love quiet evenings by the fire, a bottle of wine, and soft music. So, we do some of both! Even though her special evenings are very different from mine, I enjoy knowing she is having a great time.

—Phil

We both love to listen to piano music. We have our favorite pianists and piano bars. It is always a treat!

—Wilma

We're wild about hockey. We have season tickets and never miss a game!

—Nan and Tom

Do you and Your Beloved have fun together?
Is there a limit on how much fun you should have?

One treat a day is enough. You don't want to overdo it.

—Bill

Well, we had a great day today. The train ride, the circus, the cotton candy and popcorn, the hot dogs, now what are we going to do tomorrow?

—Alexandra

We have been married thirty years and we still date. Sometimes it's just a walk around the neighborhood; other times it's dinner or a movie. It helps to get away from the clutter and focus on each other.

—Dorothy

List five activities you consider fun.

1.

2.

3.

4.

5.

I thought we were going to have a romantic afternoon canoeing on the lake, talking, laughing, and relaxing. He challenged another couple to race across the lake and back. My romantic afternoon dissolved into an athletic event.

—Debbie

The sun was setting in Hawaii. I asked him to walk along the shoreline with me. He was too busy exercising in the gym. I walked by myself.

—Miriam

List five activities Your Beloved considers fun.

1.

2.

3.

4.

5.

> He was a tennis pro. I had never played tennis. To please him, I agreed to learn how to play. When I showed up at the tennis court in heels, tube dress, makeup, and jewelry, he stalked off the court.
>
> —Eloise

Are any of the activities you listed also on Your Beloved's list?

Do you and Your Beloved agree on ways to have fun? What are they?

> She loves to hike through the countryside. I'd rather play golf. She loves to shop. I'd rather work on my old Mustang. But we both love to eat! So we go to restaurants often.
>
> —Ed

List five shared activities.

1.

2.

3.

4.

5.

> We love to prowl in second hand stores and flea markets for antiques that we restore together. Over the years, we have made some amazing finds.
>
> —Sam

Circle those activities you will do together to have fun:

Dancing, boating, swimming, motorcycle riding, attending sports events, playing golf or cards, shopping,
hiking, skiing, bowling, cooking, walking, attending movies, plays or concerts, finding antiques,
gardening, going out to eat, ordering carry-out food and a video, reading aloud to each other,
going to museums or art galleries, hearing a lecture, learning a craft or skill, working on a project, giving a massage,
making love, paragliding, building sand castles, rock climbing, weight lifting, jogging, washing the cars, mowing the lawn, camping.

Are there other activities you will add to this list? Are you both willing to learn a new sport or skill together? What would you choose to learn? What if Your Beloved were better than you?

1.

2.

3.

It is very important for couples to play together, both while you are dating and after you are married. Many married couples still plan dates at least once a week.

Recreational activities are particularly important to build friendships and to enhance a marriage. Many couples get married so that they won't ever feel lonely again and so they will always have someone to play with.

It can be as inexpensive as laughing over the comics and doing the crossword puzzle, or a walk around the neighborhood with the dog, or as expensive as a cruise through the Mediterranean.

Play together!

Chapter 41

Dream Vacations

Describe your/Your Beloved's dream vacation.

Have you discussed this with each other?

Definitely my dream vacation is to canoe down a remote river, hike into a forested area (carrying the canoe of course) and sleep under the stars. A little fishing, a little hunting. Bliss! Her dream vacation is a trip to Paris, luxurious hotel, croissants and hot chocolate in bed, delicious dinners at swank restaurants, the Louvre, and shopping.

—Dave

We took a long bicycling tour together through Nova Scotia. To this day, it remains one of our most cherished memories.

—Lois

Have you spent at least a week's vacation together without day-to-day interruptions?

Did you become grumpy or irritable with each other? Why?

Did you run out of things to talk about?

Did you learn anything about each other that you didn't already know?

How does this new information affect your relationship?

> He took his cell phone, lap top, and dictaphone on our vacation. While I was enjoying the sights, he was working.
> —Gail

> I am not a frontiers-woman! I require a shower with hot water, a bed with a mattress, air conditioning, and no bugs. Our venture into the woods was a disaster.
> —Opheila

> The mother-in-law always accompanies us on holidays. She complains constantly about the meals, the accommodations, the kids. After two days of this, I start yelling at her and end up with a migraine headache. Who needs vacations?
> —Paula

Do you need the constant interruptions of work, friends, and family in order to tolerate Your Beloved?

> I love the beach and spend hours sunbathing, walking along the surf, or swimming in the ocean. He hates the beach, the sand, the heat, the sun, the sticky suntan lotion, and the ocean damp. Finally, he holes up in the hotel room and only ventures out for meals.
> —Marion

> I agreed to a week of camping with him. It rained, the tent leaked, the food was raw or burned, the air mattresses were forgotten. I fell and cut my knee. I got eaten by mosquitoes. I stuck a fishhook in my thumb. Every bone in my body ached from hiking or canoeing. He told me how proud he was that I came with him. I've agreed to go next year; it can't rain every day, can it?
> —Alma

> We decided to tour Italy. Neither of us could speak Italian. We missed our train. Our money was stolen. The embassy was closed for holiday. We spent the night in the church vestibule and waited until morning. He was calm, caring, and resourceful. I felt loved and protected. We still laugh about all the mishaps!
> —Taylor

It was a magic week on board ship. I don't remember much about the cruise; I just remember how much I enjoyed being with her.

—Dale

So here we were on our dream vacation. What a nightmare! He spent the entire time ogling other women, drinking at the bar and gambling.

—Ginger

What a holiday! We were biking down the side of the mountain when I lost control and flew over the edge. I broke my collarbone. He patiently and lovingly took care of me.

—Julia

Without the interruptions and the stress of everyday living, many clues about your future together will be revealed. One couple was encouraged by their marriage counselor to spend uninterrupted vacation time together before marriage.

"It's amazing what is overlooked in a dating relationship."

After spending this time together, carefully evaluate what you have learned.

Is Your Beloved still your best choice?

MARRIAGE WORKS!

Chapter 42

Work Together

Have you ever built, restored or decorated anything together? Did you finish the project?

> There are projects all over the house: the walkway, the downstairs floor, the painting, the garden, the garage. There are supplies and tools everywhere and nothing is finished.
>
> —Louise

Were you pleased with the results?

Did you become angry with each other or see the finished project differently?

Will you willingly undertake another project with Your Beloved?

> We couldn't move the couch from one end of the living room to the other without a huge argument!
>
> —Harry

> He bought the house unfinished. He planned to help me but I did all the work: drywall, plastering, carpentry work, painting, tiling, carpet-laying, landscaping. Our project quickly became my project.
>
> —Adele

> His idea of a quality job was really different from mine. I was willing to accept a lower standard than he was. Now I enjoy his extra effort knowing that whatever he does will be beautifully done!
>
> —Lilly

> We put wooden shutters into the misshapen window casings of a very old colonial house. He insisted on measuring to 1/32 of an inch! And then we painted them. Never again!
>
> —Denise

It is as important to be able to work together as it is to play together. Working together tests your communication skills!

If you see the project differently than Your Beloved, it is wise to discuss it before all the supplies are purchased. If you are working on a large project, it may help for each of you to be responsible for individual jobs rather than both working on the same job. If one of you is more skilled, one should be a willing student and the other a patient teacher.

Once the job is completed, be sure to celebrate!

Chapter 43

Acts of Kindness

Do you/Your Beloved practice random acts of kindness?

> He brings me a cup of hot chocolate every morning before he leaves for work.
>
> —Jane

> She makes my favorite dessert—cherry pie!
>
> —Al

> Hugs, anytime!
>
> —Agnes

Gifts are a delightful way to show your love; what gifts do you consider special?

Do you enjoy flowers, candy, jewelry, play tickets, sports tickets, clothes, books or dining out?

Don't expect Your Beloved to read your mind. Give Your Beloved a wish list. Know Your Beloved's favorite colors, authors, or entertainers, and his or her sizes. Surprise Your Beloved with a gift just because he or she is special to you!

List five gifts you would like to receive that cost almost nothing.

1.
2.
3.
4.
5.

I asked for a love letter. It was the best gift I have ever received.

—Jane

After a long day at work, he gives me a neck and shoulder massage.

—LuAnn

He has the house cleaned and my dinner ready when I get home.

— Melinda

We have been married twenty-two years and he still tucks love notes under my pillow, in my pockets, and books.

—Tommi

My list includes backrubs, bringing home Chinese food when I have a hard day, lattes in bed, driving more slowly, playing my favorite music, sitting together to watch the sunset, reading to me.

—Gina

How much do you think should be spent on a gift?

What is your limit? $______. Your Beloved's? $______.

List five $25.00 gifts you would like to receive.

1.
2.
3.
4.
5.

List five $50.00 gifts you would like to receive.

1.
2.
3.
4.
5.

Be sure that Your Beloved has a copy of these lists.

My husband carried around my wish list for years. Eventually, he gave me everything listed!

—Karen

Are there any occasions that demand a gift?
What are they?
Have you told Your Beloved?

I demand to be wined, dined, and gifted on Valentine's Day. Anything less than a showering of attention is unacceptable.

—Harriet

There were so many gifts that it took two days to open all the Christmas presents.

—Stan

My wedding anniversary is very important to me. Once we celebrated with a trip to Hawaii.

—Ron

If I didn't remind him for weeks, he would forget my birthday, our anniversary, and Valentine's Day.

—Louise

I was tired of receiving power tools for my birthday, so I left pictures of negligees all over the house. We both enjoyed that gift.

—Marie

Gifts do not have to be expensive. Compliments, hugs, love notes, doing Your Beloved's chores, planning for time together, or making a favorite meal, will deepen your relationship with Your Beloved.

All these actions tell Your Beloved that he or she is appreciated and loved.

These thoughtful actions will increase your love for each other and smooth the path of a lifetime commitment.

MARRIAGE WORKS!

Chapter 44

Bless This Home

Once you are married, where are you going to live?

> I love the big city. She loves her small hometown. I hate it. Two years ago she announced that she wanted to go home.
>
> —Andrew

> He inherited the family ranch. I was stunned when he decided to become a rancher. I told him, "But it's in the middle of nowhere!"
>
> —Cari

Will you move to a new city?

> I left my house and career in D.C. and moved into his family home in NYC. His mother lived a block away.
>
> —Faith

Will you move in with Your Beloved?
Will Your Beloved move in with you?
Are you already living together?
Will you move in with your in-laws?
Or will your in-laws move in with you?

While we finished our schooling, we lived in his folks' basement. They were pleasant and non-intrusive but we couldn't wait to have our own place.

—Ida

Her mother came from South America for the wedding and never left. Finally, I told her either your mother leaves or I do.

—James

Will you give up your separate homes and find a new apartment or house together?

How will you furnish your new home?

If you each have furniture and appliances, have you sorted through your belongings to decide what you will use?

What do you plan to do with the extras?

We had doubles of everything: coffee makers, toasters, blenders, televisions, dining room sets, couches, and beds. So we had a huge garage sale and bought a few new pieces of furniture together with the profits.

—Barry

Do you or Your Beloved have a collection of (whatever) and will this collection fit into your new home?

Hank collects vintage cars, trucks, tractors, and motorcycles. At last count there were more than nineteen.

—Danielle

Anna collects cats. She only had nine until one had kittens. Now she has fourteen.

—Joseph

Edward collects books. With more than 1,000 volumes, he continues to add to his collection.

—Sandy

Do you have similar tastes in furniture: modern, antique, early bachelor, Good Will, in-law donations?

Do you plan to buy new furnishings for your home? Have you agreed on a color scheme?

She moved into my home and promptly redecorated it, throwing out perfectly good fixtures, appliances, linoleum, and rugs. She said, "Your first wife's taste and mine are very different."

—Matthew

Everything was brown. "It doesn't show dirt!" His favorite chair was from Goodwill. The end tables had cigarette burns and beer can rings. He loved it all and didn't want to part with any of it. "So what's wrong with it anyway?"

—Iris

We didn't own very much: an orange porch rocker, an antique trunk, a small coffee table, a straight back chair, and a few oil paintings. After two weeks of bedrolls on the hard apartment floor, we finally decided to buy a mattress!

—Rachael

My furniture is valuable French antiques; his is ultra modern glass and chrome. Just how am I supposed to blend that?

—Angela

My favorite color is pink. The couch and carpet are pink. The dining room chairs are upholstered in pink. The kitchen curtains are pink. The bedroom has pink- flowered wallpaper.

—Barbie

If you dislike the big city, if you don't wish to live with in-laws, if you are unwilling to give up your job and move, if you don't want all your treasures stored in the basement, you must discuss these issues with Your Beloved.

Avoid surprises!

Know where your home together will be and how it will be furnished before you get married.

MARRIAGE WORKS!

Chapter 45

Chores:
If I Clean The Bathroom, Then You Do the Laundry

Have you discussed responsibility for household chores?

If both of you are working, have you agreed to split the chores?

If you are not working outside the home, do you think it is fair that you do the majority of the household chores?

> He agreed to do all the outside and garage work: lawn, car repair and maintenance, snow removal; I agreed to do the inside work: cooking, cleaning, laundry, kids.
>
> —Pia

> Sure we divided the chores. First I do mine and then I do his.
>
> —Jonnie

> My dad never did any household chores. I was stunned when my fiancé did dishes, ran the vacuum, and took out the garbage. I love that man!
>
> —Sophie

She is an awful housekeeper. Her mother is even worse. The gas company refused to hook up the stove because there was so much grease on it that it was a fire hazard.

—Curt

Have you discussed who will do which chores?

Put your initials beside the household chores you and Your Beloved have agreed to do. If you plan to do them together, put both your initials beside the chore. Set a schedule for these chores: daily, weekly, every two weeks, monthly.

1. Cooking
2. Shopping for food
3. Washing/drying dishes
4. Cleaning kitchen
5. Cleaning bathroom
6. Dusting furniture
7. Vacuuming carpets
8. Scrubbing floors
9. Changing bedding
10. Washing/Drying laundry
11. Ironing laundry
12. Washing/waxing car
13. Mowing lawn
14. Raking leaves/snow removal/gardening
15. Cleaning pet poop, fish tanks, animal cages
16. Anything else?

If the chores are not done, what are the consequences?

Do you plan to hire a cleaning service? A cook? A gardener? If so, add these initials to your household chore list.

Are you neat, a pack rat, a slob? Is Your Beloved?

Will you agree that the one with the lowest tolerance for dirt, mess, and clutter should be the one to clean it up?

Discuss this!

> We have a chore list and everything that needs to be done is written on it. We have always divided the chores equally.
>
> —Jules

> I used to give him tests. You know, leave things out and expect him to see them and put them away. Well, he is physically unable to see clutter. I got tired of stumbling over it.
>
> —Phylis

> My husband starts shedding clothes as soon as the front door is closed: boots on the stairs, socks on the landing, coat over the banister, shirt and tie on the dining room chair, wallet, glasses and books on the kitchen counter.
>
> —Olive

Or do you and Your Beloved agree with the old saying, "A place for everything and everything in its place?"

> My husband scientifically arranged the refrigerator according to size, accessibility, and perishability. No other arrangement is allowed.
>
> —Nina

> My wife arranges her spices in alphabetical order.
>
> —Stewart

> Socks have to be rolled and placed by color in the sock drawer. Boxer shorts and undershirts are ironed and folded in fours. Shirts are hung by color and collar type. Ties are sorted by color and season. Suits, sports jackets, slacks are arranged in outfits.
>
> —Leslie

Chores: whose turn it is or who didn't do them creates hard feelings. Discuss chores now, settle on an equal division of the work and agree on suitable repercussions if the chores are not done.

One couple felt so strongly that a list of chores and who was responsible for doing them was included in their wedding vows!

"Do you, my dear, agree to clean the bathroom every first and third weekend? I do!"

MARRIAGE WORKS!

Chapter 46

Kissing Don't Last. Cooking Do!

Have you eaten numerous meals with Your Beloved?
Are your eating habits and preferred foods similar?
Are you willing to accommodate differences in eating styles?

She ate ice cream every morning for breakfast.

—Evan

She ate bunny food—six small snacks a day. I was always starving. Where were the meat and potatoes?

—Joseph

He was on a special low sodium, low fat diet. I missed fried chicken, salted peanuts and desserts!

—JoyAnn

He eats one meal a day!

—Hannah

What is Your Beloved's favorite dessert? Drink?
What is Your Beloved's favorite breakfast?
Lunch? Dinner?
What are Your Beloved's favorite fruits and vegetables?

If a medical condition requires it, are you willing to prepare special diet foods?

Does Your Beloved like to eat a wide variety of foods, including ethnic foods: Chinese, Japanese, Indian, Thai, Italian, Greek, Mexican?

> We both love sushi!
>
> —Matthew

> He only ate beef and potatoes, no casseroles, soups, salads, fruit, or other vegetables. Just beef and potatoes!
>
> —Sandy

> She eats "white" foods but not "green" foods. I eat "green" foods but not "white" foods. Was this a match made in heaven?
>
> —Edgar

> None of the foods on his plate could touch. He expected two types of meat and four vegetables for dinner, and there had to be a baked dessert. Boxed cookies or canned fruit wouldn't do.
>
> —Cynthia

Are you or Your Beloved a good cook?

> He is a chef; I am his sous chef. Every meal is a gourmet treat!
>
> —Lilly

> I love to cook so I do all the cooking! And she cleans up.
>
> —John

> Her idea of cooking dinner is to buy salad in a bag, bottled salad dressing, chicken from the rotisserie, and frozen baked potatoes. If she can't nuke it, we don't eat. I'm not complaining. I'm not willing to cook!
>
> —Dan

She can't boil water without burning it.

—Fred

His mom used a French gourmet cookbook. My mom used Betty Crocker. His mom never used canned or frozen ingredients and made all her own breads, sauces, and desserts from scratch. Help!

—Betty

Kissing don't last. Cooking do!

—Old Pennsylvania Dutch Saying

Do you plan to share the cooking or help with the meal preparation?

He never says "Hi" or "How was your day?" His greeting is, "What are we having for dinner, if anything?" No matter what I tell him, he always says, "Great. That's my favorite."

—Meredith

She's the wife. She does all the cooking. It's a gender-thing, isn't it?

—Benny

Sure I cook too. I make hamburgers that have been affectionately called "hockey pucks." And I make a great frozen pizza.

—Buck

He gets home first and always starts dinner.

—Elaine

We both like to cook but we don't like to share. The house has two complete kitchens: two ovens, two sinks, two microwaves, two refrigerators, two sets of kitchen utensils. Now we're both happy.

—Anya

If you aren't the cook, do you always compliment the chef and help to clean up?

I held my breath while he ate, wondering what he would find fault with this time. If the dinner were perfect, he would complain that the coffee wasn't hot enough.

—Martha

He wanted five-star restaurant service in his own home. You know the drill: table cloth, cloth napkins, bread and butter plates, salad forks, chilled glasses. When I didn't heat the plates so that the waffles cooled too fast, he complained.

—Doris

He always tells me how delicious everything is and thanks me for spending the time to make it!

—Jody

She always says that any meal she doesn't have to cook is delicious.

—Darell

Have you ever cooked a meal together?

The first meal he cooked was a salmon soufflé. It was delicious. He made enough food for an army. We invited everyone in the apartment complex to help us eat it.

—Lydia

Have you entertained your families or your friends? Did Your Beloved help in planning the meal?

We invited his boss and his wife to dinner. I picked a bouquet of peonies for the table. While we were eating, little tiny ants climbed out of the flowers and started marching across the white tablecloth. I kept moving the serving dishes around to trap them.

—Delores

After his friends arrived, I learned that they were teatotalers. I agonized the entire time we ate the beef stew made with beer. When she told me it was delicious and asked for the recipe, I thought I'd faint.

—Sally

It was the first time his folks came for dinner. I made cherry ice cream pie. The frozen cherries rolled all over the plate and when stabbed, they jumped off the plate and bounced down the table.

—Mildred

Have you shared favorite family recipes?

I complimented my mother-in-law on the delicious dessert and when I asked for the recipe, she said, "Oh my no. I only share my recipes with family."

—Sidney

His mom gave me all his favorite recipes and taught me how to make them. Now he says my cooking is even better than his mom's cooking.

—Zelda

I made his favorite cake for his birthday, an ice cream angel food cake. I bought the angel food cake, sliced it horizontally, put ice cream between the layers, and covered the whole thing with whip cream and put it in the refrigerator. When it was time for dessert, the ice cream had melted and cake chunks were floating in the liquid. He got out bowls and spoons and served up his birthday cake. He told me it was delicious! (Now I know it goes into the freezer.)

—Belle

Do you or Your Beloved eat fast foods regularly?
Or skip meals often?

How often do you or Your Beloved eat at restaurants?
Do you eat out weekly, monthly, or only on special occasions?
Will this change after you are married?

We always go out to dinner to celebrate special occasions, birthdays, and anniversaries. We even make up special dates, like Missing Sock Day, Bone Chilling Cold Day, We Need Cheering Up Day.

—Luke

MARRIAGE WORKS!

> We really couldn't afford to go out to eat. So on our first anniversary, he put on music, lit candles, and pretended to be the waiter. Then he would hustle around to his own seat. It was delightful!
>
> —Polly

Make a list of your and Your Beloved's 5 favorite restaurants.

Share this list with Your Beloved.

1.

2.

3.

4.

5.

When I was first married, my culinary accomplishments were limited to heating frozen chicken pot pies and making Jell-O.

The main reason I am a better cook now is that my husband always complimented me on my cooking! (Following their Dad's example, my sons compliment me too!)

Whether you are vegetarians, steak and potatoes people, gourmet eaters, constant dieters, or soy protein shake drinkers, do not criticize the cook!

Chapter 47

Until Death Do You Part

Are you beginning this marriage with doubts, secrets or a hidden agenda?

> I really didn't like him very much, but I knew my parents would approve.
>
> —Marilyn

> After getting drunk and going to bed with her, she got pregnant. I had to marry her.
>
> —Bill

> He was the high school heartthrob. All my girl friends fought over him. I married him to beat them, not because I loved him.
>
> —Darlene

> I decided to marry him until someone better came along.
>
> —Ava

I married him because I thought that he was the best I could do.

—Nan

I couldn't believe that she agreed to marry me. She is gorgeous. I am nothing special. I know she will leave me for someone else.

—Steve

I met her when she was separated from her husband and fell in love with her. We married as soon as her divorce was final. I knew it was too soon for her to start a serious relationship.

—Ken

Before the wedding vows are exchanged, have other promises been made?

Can these promises be kept?

If these promises aren't kept, will that damage or destroy the marriage?

Will you be able to discuss the broken promise with Your Beloved?

I have a real dislike for fat women. My fiancée promised me that she would never get fat. And she has kept this promise.

—Johnny

His dad died of lung cancer from smoking. He promised that he would stop smoking. He hasn't stopped yet.

—Delores

He promised me that I would always live near my folks. Then the corporation moved him to the West Coast. I felt betrayed.

—Helen

He told me he was through fooling around. He said, "You're the only woman I want." He was having an affair during our engagement and several while we were married.

—Ethel

Are there any hidden agendas here?

Have you kept any secrets from Your Beloved?

Are you planning to discuss these secrets before you marry?

Are you convinced that if Your Beloved knew the truth about you, the wedding would be called off?

How likely is Your Beloved to find out these secrets?

How will Your Beloved feel once he or she knows this secret?

If found out, will these secrets damage or destroy your marriage?

My wife is bisexual.

—Hal

My wife is anorexic.

—Sidney

My husband is a cross dresser.

—Julie

My husband has a prison record.

—Agnes

My husband was married six times.

—Debbie

My husband has an illegitimate daughter he wants to raise.

—Jan

My wife had an affair with my best friend.

—Bob

My mother-in-law committed suicide; she didn't die of cancer.

—Edna

My husband is diagnosed as manic-depressive.

—Bertha

My wife has had two abortions. She is unable to bear children.

—John

My husband is addicted to gambling.

—Natalie

My fiancé wears a toupee.

—Muffie

My husband is an heir to an estate worth millions.

—Trish

My husband doesn't want children.

—Brenda

My father-in-law is an alcoholic.

—Carole

My in-laws will be living with us.

—Bert

Her brother is mentally ill.

—Jim

My fiancée has genital herpes.

—Bobbie

My husband plans to leave his lucrative job as a doctor and become a medical missionary in Africa.

—Jill

My fiancé is addicted to heroin.

—Donna

My wife is thousands of dollars in debt.

—Eric

My fiancé was fired from his job for stealing.

—Josephine

My nose was bobbed, my teeth capped, and my boobs enlarged.

—Suzy

Would you or Your Beloved consider ending your relationship for any reason; for example, infidelity, physical illness, abuse, lies?

List your reasons.

1.

2.

3.

4.

List Your Beloved's reasons.

1.

2.

3.

4.

> I told him if he ever hit me, I would leave him. It has never been an issue.
>
> —Judy

> After agreeing NOT to have an open marriage, my husband hit 40 and the seven-year itch the same year. He told me he loved me but he wanted a relationship with another woman too. No way! After a two-year separation, we resolved this and are still married.
>
> —Tyra

> I knew he had been in rehab twice for alcohol, drugs, and gambling addictions. I knew he was unfaithful. I knew he had a demanding ex and several needy children. I knew he wasn't a committed Christian. I knew my folks and friends didn't like him. I knew this would be a bad choice.
>
> —Danielle

> I told him if he weren't willing to commit to me forever, he shouldn't marry me...there would be no divorce.
>
> —Abby

Do you both agree that these reasons are serious enough to end your relationship?

Are any of these reasons likely to occur between you and Your Beloved?

Discuss these reasons with Your Beloved.

More advice from the V.O.R.:

(1) Never date someone you would be ashamed to bring home to your mother.

(2) Never make or extract promises that can't be kept.

(3) Never keep secrets from Your Beloved; no matter how long it takes, expect to be caught.

(4) Avoid future surprises by answering the questions in this book about Your Beloved.

(5) Do not marry Your Beloved if you can't commit to a lifetime marriage. And:

(6) If, after answering the questions and reading the stories in this book and listening to the advice of the V.O.R., you aren't convinced that Your Beloved is your best choice, DO NOT GET MARRIED!

Chapter 48

Your Best Choice For A Lifetime Marriage

Take every precaution now to ensure that issues that may endanger your marriage will never arise!

Agree to attend premarital counseling!

Agree that this marriage is "forever" no matter what!

Agree now to go to counseling if problems arise after you are married!

If you or Your Beloved have doubts about the future of your marriage after answering these questions, reading these stories, and listening to the V.O.R., postpone your wedding.

Decide if your concerns might lead to a future divorce. Sign up now for premarital counseling.

Plan on working together to make your future marriage last forever!

MARRIAGE WORKS!
BEFORE YOU SAY "I DO"
TEST

How to take this test:

Assess Your Beloved by placing a check mark in the appropriate column based on the subject of each chapter.

"BEST CHOICE" is self-explanatory.

"QUESTIONS" means that you have found questions raised by the chapter that only Your Beloved can answer.

"NOT MY BEST CHOICE" means that you have determined that Your Beloved fell short on the chapter's subject.

	BEST CHOICE	QUESTIONS	NOT MY BEST CHOICE
Your Best Choice			
Know Basic Facts			
Lifelong Partner			
Priorities			
Equality			
Compatibility			
Childhood			
Parents			
Mama's Boy			
Daddy's Girl			
In-Laws			
Ethnic Diversity			
Plans for Child			
Raising Child			
Money			
Budget			
Retirement			
Work			
Sex			
Prior Sex			
Prior Marriages			
Religion			

	BEST CHOICE	QUESTIONS	NOT MY BEST CHOICE
Sickness/Health			
Lifestyle			
Addictions			
WYSIWYG			
Stressed			
Communication			
Anger			
Fair Fighting			
Abusive Actions			
Mental Health			
Criminal Past			
Siblings/Friends			
Play Together			
Vacations			
Work Together			
Acts of Kindness			
Home			
Chores			
Cooking			
Secrets/Promises			

If you have numerous check marks in the "Questions" column, be sure to get your questions answered before you marry.

If you have numerous check marks in the "Not My Best Choice" column, please reconsider. This is not your best choice!

Marriage Works! Before You Say "I Do" is a collection of stories that were told to me by many men and women. If you would like to send your stories to me too, please fill out the questionnaire and mail it to me at Marriage Works!, 1153 Bergen Parkway, Ste#M352, Evergreen, Colorado, 80439-9501 or answer the questionnaire on my web site at www.marriagewks.com.

QUESTIONNAIRE

Three million weddings are performed every year, but up to 50 percent end in divorce. Why? What did or didn't you know about Your Beloved that enhanced or endangered your marriage? Join in this nationwide survey by answering the following questions. Please know that your stories (under an assumed name) may be published in my book or used by me in other public forums.

First Name ____________________ Age ______

Occupation ____

Years Married (1st) _____ (2nd) _____ (3rd) _____ (4th) ______

1. What do you wish you had known about Your Beloved before you married (for example, culture, religion, personal values, compatibility, finances, sex, health, in-laws, occupation, children, hobbies, friends, likes, dislikes)?

2. How did this lack of knowledge affect your marriage?

3. If you had known this, would you have married anyway? Why?

4. Were there any clues that you ignored?

5. What questions should be asked to get the answers you want?

If you are willing to be interviewed, please include your phone number.

Thank you!

MARRIAGE WORKS!

Bibliography

Arp, Claudia and David Arp, *10 Great Dates to Energize Your Marriage*, Michigan, Zondervan, 1997.

Beck, Aaron, *Love is Never Enough: How Couples Can Overcome Misunderstandings, Resolve Conflicts, And Solve Relationship Problems Through Cognitive Therapy*, New York, Harper & Row Publishers, Inc., 1989.

Bennett, William, *The Broken Hearth, Reversing the Moral Collapse of the American Family,* New York, Doubleday, 2001.

Bible, The NIV Study Bible, Michigan, Zondervan, 1985.

Burkett, Larry, *The Complete Financial Guide for Young Couples*, Illinois, Victor Books, 1989.

Buscaglia, Leo, *Love: What Life Is All About*, New York, Ballantine Books, 1972.

Chavez, Linda, "Making Marriage Work," *The Denver Post*, May 31, 2000 at 11B.

Clark, Beverly, *All About Her: A Personal Reference From the Woman in My Life*, Illinois, Marcella L. Jaegle, 1995.

Clephane, Ellen, *Dance of Love: What Fifty Couples Say Makes Their Relationships Really Work,* Element Books Ltd., 1996.

Coleman, Paul, *30 Secrets of Happily Married Couples,* Massachusetts, Adams Media Corporation, 1992.

Corn, Laura, *237 Intimate Questions Every Woman Should Ask a Man,* California, Park Avenue Publishers, 2000.

DeAngelis, Barbara, *Are You the One for Me?: Knowing Who's Right and Avoiding Who's Wrong,* New York, Dell Publishing, 1992.

DeAngelis, Barbara, *The 100 Most Asked Questions About Love, Sex, and Relationships,* New York, Random House Audio, 1997.

DiPietro, Joe (book and lyrics), and Jimmy Roberts (music), *I Love You, You're Perfect, Now Change*, Hal Leonard Corporation, New York, 1996.

Dobson, James, *What Wives Wish Their Husbands Knew About Women*, Illinois, Tyndale House Publishers, Inc., 1975.

Fisher, Bruce and Robert Alberti, *Rebuilding When Your Relationship Ends,* California, Impact Publishers, Inc., 1999.

Forget Paris, Copyright © 1995 Columbia Pictures.

Four Weddings and a Funeral, Copyright © 1994 Gramercy Pictures.

Gallagher, Maggie, *The Abolition of Marriage: How We Destroy Lasting Love,* District of Columbia, Regnery Publishing, 1996.

Galston, William, "Rethinking Divorce," *Center of the American Experiment*, April 1996.

The Godfather, Copyright © 1972 Paramount Pictures.

Gottman, John, *Why Marriages Succeed or Fail: And How You Can Make Yours Last,* New York, Simon & Schuster, 1995.

Gottman, John, *A Couple's Guide to Communication*, Illinois, Research Press, 1979.

Groundhog Day, Copyright © 1993 Columbia Pictures.

Harley, Willard, *Love Busters: Overcoming Habits That Destroy Romantic Love,* Michigan, Revell Co., 2002.

Harley, Willard, *His Needs, Her Needs,* Michigan, Revell Co., 1986.

The Heritage Foundation Backgrounder, "The Child Abuse Crisis: The Disintegration of Marriage, Family, and the American Community," June 3, 1997.

Hochschild, Arlie, *Second Shift,* New York, Penguin, 1989.

Hollander, Dory, *101 Lies Men Tell Women: And Why Women Believe Them*, New York, HarperCollins Publishers, 1997.

Horn, Ph.D. Wade, "Fear of divorce keeps many from marriage," *The Washington Times*, April 12, 1998, at 30.

Hybels, Bill and Lynne Hybels, *Fit To Be Tied,* Michigan, Zondervan Publishing House, 1991.

Kaminer, Wendy, *I'm Dysfunctional, You're Dysfunctional: The Recovery Movement and Other Self-Help,* New York, Vintage, 1993.

Klagsbrun, Francine, *Married People: Staying Together in the Age of Divorce,* New York, Bantam, 1985.

Knapp, Caroline, *Drinking: A Love Story*, New York, The Dial Press, 1996.

Knight, Al, "Fighting to preserve marriage," *The Denver Post*, May 17, 2000, at 11B.

Kreidman, Ellen, *Light His Fire: How to Keep Your Man Passionately and Hopelessly In Love With You,* New York, Dell, 1991.

Kreidman, Ellen, *Light Her Fire: How to Ignite Passion, Joy, and Excitement in the Women You Love,* New York, Dell, 1992.

Littauer, Florence, *Your Personality Tree,* Dallas, Word Publishing, 1986.

Littauer, Florence, *Personality Plus,* Michigan, Fleming H. Revell, 1983.

Louden, Jennifer, *The Couple's Comfort Book: Creative Guide for Renewing Passion, Pleasure, and Commitment,* New York, HarperCollins Publishers, 1993.

Markman, Ph.D. Howard and Scott Stanley, and Susan Blumberg, *Fighting for Your Marriage,* San Francisco, Jossey-Bass Publishers, 1994.

McCann, Graham, *Cary Grant*, New York, Columbia University Press, 1996.

McGeady, Mary Rose, *Are You Out There, God?* New York, Covenant House, 1996.

Morton, Andrew, *Diana: Her True Story—In Her Own Words*, New York, Simon & Schuster, 1997. Excerpts reprinted in "Camilla's Specter Casts a Shadow on Diana's Future," *The Denver Post*, November 11, 1997.

Notarius,Ph.D. Clifford, and Ph.D. Howard Markman, *We Can Work It Out: Making Sense of Marital Conflict,* Putnam Pub Group, 1993.

Pearsall, Ph.D. Paul, *The Ten Laws of Lasting Love*, New York, Simon & Schuster, 1993.

Prather, Hugh, *I Will Never Leave You,* New York, Bantam, 1995.

Rocky Mountain News, "Children of divorce more likely to smoke and drink, study shows," September 12, 1998, at 53A.

Rocky Mountain News, "The Despair of a Promise Keeper's Wife," October 29, 1997, at 46A.

Rosenthal, Neil, "Heart Too Hasty Right After Divorce," *The Denver Post*, November 20, 1997 at 2E.

Samenow, Stanton, *Before It's Too Late: Why Some Kids Get Into Trouble – and What Parents Can Do About It*, New York, Three Rivers Press, 2001.

Schlessinger, Laura, *How Could You Do That?!: The Abdication of Character, Courage, and Conscience,* New York, Harper Paperbacks, 1997.

Shapiro, Joan and George Hartlaub, *Men: A Translation for Women*, New York, EP Dutton, 1992.

Smalley, Gary and John Trent, *The Two Sides of Love*, California, Focus on the Family Publishing, 1990.

Smalley, Gary, *Making Love Last Forever,* Dallas, Word Publishing, 1996.

Stanley, Scott, *A Lasting Promise: A Christian Guide to Fighting for Your Marriage,* New York, Jossey-Bass, 1998.

Wallerstein, Judith and Sandra Blakeslee, *The Good Marriage: How and Why Love Lasts*, New York, Warner Books, 1996.

Wallerstein, Judith and Julia Lewis and Sandra Blakeslee, *The Unexpected Legacy of Divorce*, New York, Hyperion, 2000.

Waite, Linda and Maggie Gallagher, *The Case for Marriage: Why Married People Are Happier, Healthier, and Better Off Financially*, New York, Doubleday, 2000.

Whitehead, Barbara, *The Divorce Culture,* New York, Alfred A. Knopf, 1997.

Wolf, Sharon, *How to Stay Lovers for Life: Discover a Marriage Counselor's Tricks of the Trade,* New York, Dutton Adult, 1997.

Index